East Coast KETO 2

more TIPS & LESSONS
TO HELP SIMPLIFY YOUR KETOGENIC LIFESTYLE

Bobbi Pike

WITH SIDEKICK
Geoff Pike

BREAKWATER
P.O. BOX 2188, ST. JOHN'S, NL, CANADA, A1C 6E6
WWW.BREAKWATERBOOKS.COM

ISBN 978-1-55081-872-7

A CIP catalogue record for this book is available from Library and Archives Canada.

We acknowledge the financial support of the Government of Canada and the Government of Newfoundland and Labrador through the Department of Tourism, Culture, Industry and Innovation for our publishing activities.

PRINTED AND BOUND IN CANADA.

Breakwater Books is committed to choosing papers and materials for our books that help to protect our environment. To this end, this book is printed on a recycled paper and other controlled sources that are certified by the Forest Stewardship Council®.

The information provided in *East Coast Keto* represents personal opinion and experience and does not replace professional medical or nutritional advice. Always consult your physician or a health-care professional before starting any nutrition or exercise program to determine if it is right for you.

Geoff and I would like to dedicate this book to my dear old Dad, Weldon Seymour.

Dad (and Mom, whom we lost in 2013) raised me to be a thinker, not a follower; to be strong and outgoing; and to never accept the unjust things about this world, but instead to respectfully speak up. He raised me to stand up to bullies and even to stand up for myself against my two big brothers when they were being a torment!

He saw in me the early stages of who I would become. He recognized the spirit and the pure gumption, a fiery quest for something more. Some parents would have tried to temper and tame that spirit, but instead he and mom helped me to hone it, and to learn to make my point with dignity, tact, and poise.

He taught me to fish, even though I didn't even like the wee smelly beasties. He's mentored me in the garden and taught me patience in watching a seed grow. He's given me his last dollar, and also showed me the value of that dollar. He understood when I wanted to be a tomboy and not the girl in the frilly dress. He instilled in me morals and values. He sacrificed for our family.

He's always been my number one fan. (Sorry, Geoff, he has had fan status for so much longer!) When we started this ketogenic journey, his support was unwavering. He had faith that even though it was different from what we were used to, we had done our research and due diligence, and would succeed in our goals. He believed in us.

Cheers to you, Dad. Thank you for being you.

First and foremost, a huge thanks to the kind folks at Breakwater for wanting to play with me again! Each and every encounter leaves me feeling ever so glad that I chose you as my dance partner for this endeavor. Much respect and love to you all.

To Jocelyne, for helping me to express my keto-correct thoughts while allowing me to keep my uniqueness, quirks and 'wild as a goat-ed-ness.' I had to sneak that 'not real' word in here, as I still can't spell keto (as in 'Ketonian' from the planet 'Keto') with a capital K in the outer and main part of the book! You are appreciated! Thank you for making it easy and fun!

To Maria E, for forging the path, for the kind words, the never-ending support, the keto guidance, and for allowing me to pick your brain. I appreciate you more than you know!

For Nicole S, for making me accountable, for being my sounding board, provider of information, and for just being uber-cool. Thank you for everything.

Sending a huge shout out to our ECK community! We keep saying it over and over again; we may be the faces of East Coast Keto, but you guys are the heart and soul, not to mention the reason that we do what we do. The outpouring of love and support is often overwhelming. You guys make all the work that goes into the social media posts, recipe development, and editing all worthwhile.

For Alex M, for always being my anchor. You have always been my most honest advisor. I know that when I ask, you will give me the straight-up answer that I need, no holds barred. Thank you for always making me want to be a better person. You are my greatest achievement and will always be the very best recipe that I have ever created.

For Samantha P, for the support and the love and for believing in us! Thank you for being the best S'daughter a gal could have. You will always have a home and safe haven where we are.

To Kayla D, thank you for the chats and the support and for holding the hand of the young feller that I love. You will always have a special place in my heart.

Gail V, you were there from the beginning and it was so much fun to grow alongside of you. We have come so far! Thank you for your guidance and support, I love every hair on your head.

Lisa B, you always knock me for a loop! Your sense of humour, wit, and easy devil-may-care attitude are right up my alley! Thank you for being a kindred spirit. P.S: I still want to be your flower girl.

Alison S, your support locally has been so appreciated! Whether it's wingman at a launch, or a friendly face at the food markets, I know you always have my back. Much love!

Carolyn T, (and Romeo) You are my early bird! Words can't describe how much I appreciate your friendly face and your support. Thank you for being you and sharing of yourself.

Diane C, your fresh keto face and dynamic personality has been such a refreshing addition. I love the way you look at life, and your willingness to help others!

Lisa FF, to our newest! Seeing your progress has been a pure pleasure and can't wait to watch your journey continue! Thank you for your kindness, compassion, and support.

G, my darling sidekick...it was always you! This journey wouldn't have happened without you. You helped me to create such a happy and stable environment that it made me want to be a better person and strive for more. You have progressed from the 'just tell me what to eat' guy, to the passionate and knowledgeable sidekick who deserves equal billing, in the kitchen and out. Please keep holding my hand and laughing with me. Come on, we goes!!!

CONTENTS

Introduction | 9

LET'S KETO | 11

HOW TO EAT YOUR MACROS | 11

CALORIES ARE NOT A CONCERN | 11

PRIORITY ONE: CUTTING CARBS | 12

PRIORITY TWO: PROTEIN–SAME AS USUAL, BUT FATTIER CUTS | 12

PRIORITY THREE: FATS–USE ONLY WHAT YOU NEED DAILY | 13

HOW DO I KEEP TRACK? | 14

HOW TO READ A FOOD LABEL | 14

IS THIS KETO? | 14

WHERE TO START | 14

TRICKY SERVING SIZES | 16

HOW TO KETO ON A BUDGET | 16

THIS ONE'S FOR THE GALS | 19

HAIR LOSS | 20

MENTAL HEALTH | 21

LET'S TALK ABOUT STRESS | 22

WHAT CAN WE DO TO IMPROVE? | 22

CARBING UP | 24

TALKING KETO ON THE ROAD | 25

LEARN TO DEFINE YOUR KETO | 25

KETOING THE CUISINES | 28

EAST COAST KETO COOKING

LISTEN TO YOUR BODY: **APPETIZERS AND SNACKS** | 30

BREAKING YOUR FAST: **BREAKFAST AND BRUNCH** | 54

LET'S DIVE IN: **SOUPS AND STEWS** | 80

LOOK TO THE SEA: **SEAFOOD** | 98

CLEAN PROTEIN: **MEAT AND POULTRY** | 120

IS PORTION CONTROL NECESSARY: **SIDES** | 162

LITTLE THINGS:**SAUCES AND EXTRAS** | 186

AN EXTRA BOOST: **FAT BOMBS** | 214

SWEET TREATS: **DESSERTS** | 232

MAD MIXOLOGY | 270

APPENDICES | 275

East Coast KETO
TIPS & LESSONS TO HELP
SIMPLIFY YOUR KETOGENIC LIFESTYLE
Bobbi Pike
Geoff Pike
THE PLACE
Gary Collins
ROALD DAHL

Introduction

We are so excited to bring you *East Coast Keto 2*! Book 2 is chock-a-block full of even more of our fave recipes turned keto, and we've got some great info on how to fine tune your keto as an intermediate ketonian.

If you're brand-spanking-new to the keto world and you're looking for info to get started, we recommend you pick up our first book, *East Coast Keto*. It will give you all the info you need to start a ketogenic lifestyle, plus all the knowledge you need to feel secure in the beginning days of your new way of eating.

Make sure you also check out our website, EastCoastKeto.com and our YouTube channel where we occasionally sneak out a top-secret recipe that's designated for our next publication. Lastly, find our Facebook community/group entitled East Coast Keto, for extra drama-free support. Most of the day-to-day answers to your questions will be provided there, but if you need extra one-on-one help, you will find our coaching packages on our website.

Let's get started!

Let's Keto

HOW TO EAT YOUR MACROS

You can find anything on the Internet these days. There are websites that guarantee that the earth is flat, people selling snake oil (that's really bottled water), or fine folks selling parcels of land that turn out to be a swamp.

This is also the case closer to home in our keto world. The Internet is full of articles on how to eat your macros. A quick google search will bring up hundreds of articles, all with differing opinions. You will stumble across tips such as "Use fats as a lever!" (What does that even mean!?!) "Make sure you get your fats in daily!" (Please don't guzzle fats.) or even "Divide your body weight by ten and then do some crazy math to determine how much water to drink!" (Drink to satisfy thirst, only!)

It's easy to overload on information. The trouble starts when you try to determine which article is offering sound advice and which is info that should be clearly avoided. Just because you read it on the Internet, doesn't mean it's so. Finding information and a source that you can trust is important.

Let's see if we can set the record straight.

CALORIES ARE NOT A CONCERN

Don't worry about calories. If you're tracking your macros you are already tracking calories! The biggest portion of a calorie is made up from macronutrients (a substance or element required in relatively large amounts to support growth and development), and micronutrients (a substance or element required in trace amounts to support growth and development). If you break a calorie apart and look at its main components, it looks like this:

CALORIES = PROTEIN + CARBS + FATS

In our keto world, our macros are our focus! Don't overwhelm yourself or let yourself get bogged down on the details.

Daily food intake and how much to eat can be simplified.

PRIORITY ONE: CUTTING CARBS

Your main concentration is to ensure your carb intake is low, and generally that translates to either Net or Total Carb (numbers given are industry standard amounts):

Net carbs is calculated as 20g of carbs daily (after subtracting fibre and sugar alcohols)

Total carbs is calculated as 50g of carbs daily (without any subtractions)

It's believed that Total Carbs gives a more accurate account of daily intake. In recent years, it's been discovered that fibre, once believed to be 100% waste and unused by the body, is in reality being at least partially digested. So, if we follow the Net Carbs theory daily, what portion of the fibre do we subtract? It's a wild card that some ketonians choose to avoid.

A sugar alcohol is a man-made sweetener, which has been derived from a natural source. An example would be erythritol, which is derived from the stevia plant.

Sugar alcohols further complicate the matter. There are two schools of thought on how to count them. Some subtract them all from the Total Carbs, and others only subtract half if the amount is over five.

For example:

TOTAL CARBS 20g − FIBRE 7g − SUGAR ALCOHOLS 10g = NET CARBS 3g

OR

TOTAL CARBS 20g − FIBRE 7g − SUGAR ALCOHOLS 5g (HALF OF 10) = NET CARBS 8g

As with the fibre, we're just not sure how much is really digested (as food) and how much is sent out of the body as waste. Our advice is to exercise caution here, and measure using half the count, as in this second example.

PRIORITY TWO: PROTEIN—SAME AS USUAL, BUT FATTIER CUTS

Your next priority after carbs would be ensuring you're getting enough protein. Generally speaking, from 60g to 110g daily is a good target.

Out of everything you eat, quality in food really matters when it comes to protein. Avoid protein shakes and processed meats, and focus on eating real meat/protein.

The rule of thumb is to eat the same amount of protein as you did in your pre-keto days, but use a fattier cut. Choose pieces of meat that have a lot of marbling, not a fatty cap. This marbled fat is full-on flavour and also helps to tenderize the meat. If using a lean meat, add butter or an alternate fat to your plate.

"Can I overeat meat? If I eat too much protein will it take me out of ketosis?" People sometimes ask this, but it should not be a concern, unless you eat massive amounts of protein daily. You would really have to eat a huge amount of protein—as in, enough for two or three people—for that to be a factor.

PRIORITY THREE: FATS—USE ONLY WHAT YOU NEED DAILY

The final priority would be to switch out those inflammatory vegetable oils and instead use healthy animal fats. Vegetable oils aren't really made from vegetables; they're seed oils that were extracted with chemicals and high heat. Avoid these inflammatory oils where possible.

The hardest part of keto is getting your head around the fat. Don't fear the fat, but don't guzzle bacon juice just to meet your macros, either. Let me explain.

Use fats only to satisfy your hunger and provide your body with a source of energy. Don't try to meet your fat macro everyday; instead, use what your body asks for, as indicated by your hunger. You shouldn't be hungry on keto. If you're hungry, eat (while still reducing carbs)! If you're thirsty, drink! It's that simple!

If you have a day where you're working in the garden or hiking, you will burn more energy. On those days your body will ask for more fuel/food. Eat!!

On the days where you are chilling on the couch watching Netflix, you're using less energy. Your body won't need as much fats/food to feel satisfied. Eat less that day!

If you're hungry, know that the fat is what keeps you feeling full. Try to incorporate healthy fats into every meal and snack.

tip **The secret to curing obesity is to cure hunger. How do you cure hunger? By incorporating healthy dietary fats.**

HOW DO I KEEP TRACK?

There are lots of great apps out there for counting daily macros. Use these apps for counting only and never to tell you what is or is not keto. It's important that you know which ingredients to avoid, the names of hidden sugars and starches, and what preservatives, additives and chemicals are in foods.

These apps will calculate your personal macros (protein, fat, and carbs) for you based on the information that you provide, such as your age, height, current weight, and activity levels. These numbers may vary slightly between apps—don't stress about this. Just pick the app that has the most pleasing and useful interface.

Be careful which food entries you choose within the apps. Not all food selections are verified by app creators, and the majority are user-submitted. If an entry seems out of whack, check another entry, or ask Google for a basic carb count for that particular food.

Pick yourself up a food scale. You can purchase them rather cheap at most department stores such as Walmart. Measure before you cook your food; cooked foods lose water weight (and some nutrients), but they don't lose calories. Weigh food raw.

HOW TO READ A FOOD LABEL

IS THIS KETO?

Many newbies start this way of life thinking that keto is just about cutting carbs, but it's so much more than that. Keto is always 'ingredients first'; if the ingredients aren't clean, then it doesn't matter what the carb count is.

Sometimes it seems like the more you know about the world of nutrition, the more you have to learn, and reading nutrition labels is no exception. Nutrition labels and ingredients play a different role, but you need to be able to read and interpret both to get the full picture.

WHERE TO START

Nutrition Labels. These contain the breakdown of what can be found in a suggested serving size. In Canada and the US, it's standard to show the measurements of all nutritional components, meaning that they will show us the protein and fibre as well as the carbs/sugars. We have to do the subtraction ourselves to calculate the values. It is also standard to show all nutritional information on the labels.

The 'but' here comes when you're dealing with a product from another country. Some countries will have the fibre already subtracted; some will show codes for additives like MSG. For example, in Britain E955 is sucralose and E621 is MSG. Every country will have its own regulations, so if you're dealing with a product from another country, best practice is to investigate and do an Internet search about that particular country's nutrition labels.

Watch for headings and subheadings here. For example, carbs would have sugars and starches below it to show the nutritional breakdown of that carb. We wouldn't count both, as the sugar and starch would be already accounted for.

Ingredients List. Think of ingredients as food items 'added' to the recipe or product. Manufacturers have to show the list of everything they add to a product. Many people get confused, especially when it comes to natural sugars. For example, tomatoes have natural sugars; it's a part of the nutritional make-up of the fruit.

If you had a can of just tomatoes, there would only be tomatoes in the ingredients list.

INGREDIENTS: TOMATOES.

Nutrition Facts

Sugars 6g — **That sugar value is the amount of natural sugar found in a tomato.**

However, if the manufacturer added **extra** sugars to that tomato, the labels would look different. Because the sugars did not occur naturally in this case, they would have to be listed as an added ingredient. So, the labels would change.

INGREDIENTS: TOMATOES, BROWN SUGAR.

Nutrition Facts

Sugars 9g — **The ingredients show there are extra things added to the recipe, which is then also reflected in the nutrition label.**

Ingredients are listed by weight, meaning the first ingredient will be what makes up most of your food item, and the last ingredient will be the item that is present in the smallest amount.

tip **If there is a list of ingredients a mile long, that's your first sign to avoid the product. Chances are those ingredients are telling the tale that the product is full of additives and preservatives. These chemicals are never a friend of any ketonian. Try to choose foods that have a very short ingredient list, and ultimately the best choice would be a food with no ingredient list, like a piece of meat, or a piece of fish.**

TRICKY SERVING SIZES

What if there is a sugar listed as an added ingredient, but it's not showing on the nutrition label?

Manufacturers will often reduce the serving size down small enough so they can show a value of less than 1. In this case, they are permitted to exclude these items from the nutrition label altogether. So, if the sugars are 0.9, they could use a zero value. Needless to say, this can quickly add up if you're unaware of this and you're using larger quantities of these foods.

For example:

WHIPPING CREAM

Nutrition Facts	
Serving Size 1 Tbsp	Carbs 0g
Serving Size 1 Cup	Carbs 7g

The serving size has been reduced here to show a value of less than 1, so the carb value is omitted. It's a manipulation of the numbers; it's not that there are no carbs here, they're just carefully hidden.

Stevia is another example of how they reduce serving sizes; for example, on packets of sweetener or on soft drinks, the carb value shows as zero. Increased exponentially, these carbs will add up. Carb creep is a real thing.

Take charge of your keto status and educate yourself on how to fully understand what you're consuming. Investigating what's in your food, in particular additives and their effect on the body, is worth the time spent. The more you work with labels and ingredient lists, the more aware you will become. With any luck we will continue to grow and learn as we progress in our keto journey, as we travel towards optimal health.

HOW TO KETO ON A BUDGET

It's a common misconception that eating a ketogenic diet is more expensive than the average Western diet, but that's not the case at all. With a few easy tips, you can be eating healthy and saving much more than you ever did before. Following is a list of how we successfully keto without breaking the bank.

Plan ahead. Make sure you're subscribed to local grocery flyers so you know what's on sale at your local store. Clip coupons and make a shopping list so you know exactly where to go to get the best deals. Apps like Flipp and Reebee are great tools here!

Join local coupon groups. Coupon groups are treasure troves of deals, especially in social media forums. Most coupon groups are terrific at sharing the deals (after they have their own stashes) so these groups will be full of found deals! This is free advice on where to get deals in your area.

Buy the deals. Even if you're not a coupon clipper, there are deals to be had. Most supermarket deals start on Thursdays, so that's a great day to visit your local store. Buy what's on sale, and if you have access to a deep freeze, buy in bulk.

Buy a vacuum sealer. A vacuum sealer is a great investment. While most kitchen tools won't make our budget keto shopping list, this small appliance will. Many of us are guilty of throwing out food, but a vacuum sealer will extend the fridge life of most foods by 3 weeks and the freezer life of your food by months. It will also save you thousands of dollars yearly in food wastage.

Buy in bulk. Get used to hitting up the wholesale shops in your area; butter, whipping creams, meats and many other staples are a great buy at wholesale clubs, but don't ever assume they are THE best deal. Sometimes the weekly specials are a much better buy. Educate yourself and be a smart shopper. Check discount stores for common ingredients, such as Himalayan pink salt, canned meats, and other keto food items. Always check ingredient lists.

Use buyers' programs. If you have a points program, make sure you sign up and use it! It's amazing how easily those points rack up. These points can usually be redeemed in store for dollars off your weekly groceries. You can often purchase gift certificates (watch for promotions!) for points and then redeem them right away for your groceries. That's free money.

Buy bigger cuts of meat. Any time a butcher (or any other person who prepares food) touches or changes a product, the price goes up. So, if a bone or skin is removed, or the product is chopped, you will be paying for that employee's time as well as the product you are buying. Process these items at home by yourself and save! It's often cheaper to buy a full chicken or turkey than it is to buy individual pieces.

Shop veggies in season. You will often find fresh vegetables on sale when they are in season. Purchase them in bulk at this time and put them aside in freezer bags, bottles, or cans for future use. Farmers' markets and vegetable stands are often great places for deals. Support local whenever possible.

Buy spices and dry ingredients in bulk. When possible, purchase spices and other dry ingredients out of bulk stores or bulk bins. Those pretty little labels and bottles you see at the grocery store will often increase the price of a spice by 300%!

Buy fattier cuts of meat. Fattier cuts of meat are often cheaper than the leaner cuts and the great news is, they're often great to add to the high-fat portion of your ketogenic diet.

Buy frozen if fresh is not on sale. We all know fresh is better, but with today's technology, the flash-freezing process locks in nutrients and saves you money to boot!

Save bones to make broth. Don't spend your money on store-bought broth when you can make your own. Boil bones for a couple of hours (see bone broth recipe in our first book, page 105) and then strain them to remove any pieces. Also save your broth (pot liquor) from a boiled dinner! You can freeze these in ice cube trays for little nuggets of flavour for your recipes.

Save bacon grease and tallow. Many ketonian kitchens have a bowl or bottle of bacon fat that has been saved throughout the week. This can be used to add fat and flavour to any meal.

Be careful of wasted food. The average North American family throws out between 25% and 40% of all food they purchase. Whether it's spoilage or unused leftover food, keep an eagle eye on this money waster. Best before dates are suggested timelines that food manufacturers use as a safety guideline; the food doesn't automatically spoil on that day. Be careful how much food you purchase, and how much you prepare.

Keep your cooking simple. Simple keto is a piece of meat or fish, healthy fats, and green and leafy veg. That's it! Cooking with specialty ingredients such as almond flour, coconut flour, sweeteners, MCT (medium-chain triglycerides) oil etc., can be a real wallet-buster and is in no way necessary to a successful keto diet. These items should not be added to any budgets when calculating keto costs; they are extras and should be cut from any penny-pinching diet.

Grow your own food. Above-ground veggie gardens and small hobby farms are a great way to reduce grocery bills, and can also provide great mental health benefits. If you don't have the space, think about a small herb window box. Gardening is known for its Zen qualities, so you'll be reaping the benefits two-fold.

Bottom line? Calculating your keto return is probably the biggest way you ARE saving on keto. When you calculate what you are saving with ketogenic living, it's a real eye opener:

Saving on clothes. Often bigger clothes in specialty stores are double if not triple the price of smaller sizes. Add to this, most of us have clothes tucked away in the back of the closet that we've grown out of. We get to pull them out and enjoy the old becoming brand-new again.

Heartburn medicines. In our past life we had a constant supply of tummy medicines within reach at all times; in the car, the office desk, and especially on the night table. Just calculating the savings on this alone would be staggering.

Reducing medicine cost. You might have co-pay insurance, but nevertheless, those meds can add up. Medications for blood pressure, diabetes, cholesterol, and inflammation (pain relief), to name a few, can be reduced or even eliminated in consultation with your doctor.

Less snack food. Let's face it, our carts were filled with chips and soft drinks and sugary snacks—so much so that they became a part of our everyday existence, and not snack foods at all. Keto keeps us full and we don't need snacks.

Expensive processed foods. Going back to basics eliminates the need for all the extras. We buy the bare-bones ingredients and make them ourselves, instead of paying someone else to do it for us. Time well spent, I think.

tip **Convenience foods, convenience stores and convenience eating; convenience has helped to make us unhealthy and fat! Learn to 'un-convenience' yourself and make your own food!**

At the end of the day, what price can you put on your health and that of your family? Even if it were more expensive, I would make cuts elsewhere to make keto a part of my life. If we don't have our health, we have nothing, and the value of our family's health? It's just priceless!!

THIS ONE'S FOR THE GALS

So, you've made the leap to keto and you're delighted with the amount of weight that you're losing. You're feeling fabulous in your skin and you're starting to feel super healthy. Then it hits: the period from hell!! Those super heavy-duty overnighters are not fitting the bill and you've been bleeding for so long that you're starting to wonder if you're gonna make it out alive!

Or maybe you've been regular your whole life and now you're two weeks late and you're starting to panic.

We feel your pain! We've all been there, wondering what the heck is going on with our body now?! Is this normal? Well, buckle your seat belts ladies, we're going to chat about lady parts, including hormones, monthly periods, and how it can affect YOU!

Let's start with hormones. Our body produces three different types of estrogen; the first, estradiol, is produced by the ovaries; these are the good guys. The second, estrone, is produced by your fat cells; these are the bad unhealthy guys. Finally, the third type, estriol, is only produced when you're pregnant. Collectively, they are known as 'estrogen hormones'.

Estrogen has a very tangled relationship with our fat. Fat cells produce estrogen, so the more fat you have, the more estrogen there is in your body. Your body, in an attempt to control the excess hormones that come with excess fat, will encapsulate the estrogen in fat and store it away. As your body burns fat/loses it through ketosis, this stored estrogen is released back into your now-healthier body and can often result in irregular bleeding. Personally, whenever I'm actively losing weight, my period acts up when it's not supposed to. This is a part of what's happening to your monthly system. Your periods can be irregular, heavier, lighter, and all over the place. Everyone's body will react differently.

tip **Your fat cells are not just composed of fat! Your body has been quietly stowing away all kinds of things it couldn't process over the years, such as pollutants, pesticides and other chemical additives. Be patient with your body as it works to heal!**

As much as we all wish there were, there is no magic pill to be found to alleviate the effects associated with menstruation. All of the things that usually happen around your period will still occur. Cramping will still make an appearance around your periods, water retention will still happen, if you were moody around your period before, it probably will still be an issue after keto...life will go on. Sore breasts and tender nipples can also be an issue as your body gets used to keto; your desire for sex can decrease or increase. Weight fluctuations will still happen and the scales will not be your friend. So be smart and just stay off the scales! Cravings for chocolate and salty food will still be a worry. Plan ahead and make sure you have an arsenal of keto-friendly options on stand-by, so you're ready for it. Don't let an unexpected craving throw you off keto.

The good news is, things will eventually return to normal as your body gets used to its new normal. Your body's natural cycle has a strong pull that ties in with the cycles of the moon. It won't lay dormant or injured for long. Also, as you get nearer to menopause, ketosis can give you a break in that aspect as well. Carbohydrates promote inflammation which leads to hormonal imbalances that lead to hot flashes. If you don't feed your body carbohydrates, there will be fewer hot flashes. I'm super thankful for this one!

HAIR LOSS

If you're losing hair, it's not because of what you're eating now; it was when you changed your diet three to six months ago. It's your body's response to an abrupt change or stress, and also occurs in people who are in car accidents or other life-changing events. You're not losing any more hair than usual, it just happens a little differently than normal, making it look like more.

THE FOUR STAGES OF HAIR GROWTH

1. ANAGEN

Growth phase, determines hair length. (two- to seven-year period) New hair is formed and begins to push the older hair up through the follicle and out. The hair grows about 1 cm every 30 days in this stage. People who have difficulty growing their hair past a certain length probably have a short growth phase, while people with long hair can thank a longer active growth phase.

2. CATAGEN

Transition phase (14-21 days). Growth stops and the outer root sheath shrinks and attaches to the root of the hair, forming what is known as a club hair. About 3% of all hairs are in this phase at a given time.

3. TELOGEN

Resting phase (three months or more) The hair follicle is resting and the club hair is completely formed. Even though the old hair is resting, a new growth phase is in the works. About 25 to 100 hairs are shed normally each day.

4. EXOGEN

The new hair phase (three months or more). As the final part of the resting phase, this is when the old hair sheds and a new hair continues to grow. Approximately 50 to 150 hairs can fall out daily in this phase; this is considered to be normal hair shedding.

That's the natural hair growth process. That's why if you have any laser treatment, you have to go back more than once, to get the new growths.

As we age, the length of the anagen stage decreases, so the hair may become weaker and thinner after each cycle. Significant stress can cause larger numbers of follicles than normal to enter the resting phase. Easing into ketosis allows your body ample time to adapt without receiving a shock. Otherwise, the best thing you can do for your hair is make sure you're enough eating good quality protein, i.e. real meat (see note below). This is one of the reasons we say no to protein shakes and meal replacements. Quality of food really matters in keto.

Collagen and biotin both help with hair growth. Collagen, which you get from meats, especially gristle and skin, will help with nails and skin repair, and biotin will thicken hair. Picture a single shaft of hair; biotin will cause it to thicken up and produce off-shoots—almost like split ends, but in a good way. Don't worry, it won't be visible; this all is microscopic. What you will notice is your hair thickening and becoming lusher. Scrubbing your head while washing (to increase blood flow) will also help encourage regrowth.

MENTAL HEALTH?

Yes!! It's a big part of keto.

I look back over life in general and my own reactions to outside stressors, and I'm always grateful for darling Sidekick Geoff's offered support, especially in times of high stress. During one such period, and a much-appreciated pep talk, he helped to put things in perspective for me. Sometimes it's normal to be stressed.

Feeling stressed? What you're feeling right now is a perfectly normal reaction to a very extraordinary situation. It's hard getting your head around the thought that some 'feelings' are completely normal to feel at certain times in life, even though it doesn't feel normal in any way. So, in reality, stressing over the validity of feelings just adds more stress to what we're already dealing with.

LET'S TALK ABOUT STRESS

Why is it a bad thing? Why should we avoid stress? Does it really have a negative impact on our lives?

Stress has been connected to many health issues, such as high blood pressure, heart disease, obesity, and diabetes, to name a few. These are also things that we try to change for the better with the help of ketogenic living. So, there has to be a connection, right?

Did you know that when you are stressed, your body responds by releasing a hormone called cortisol? In a happy world where our body is functioning normally, cortisol can help control blood sugar levels, regulate metabolism, help reduce inflammation, and assist with memory formulation. It has a controlling effect on salt and water balance and helps control blood pressure. All good things, right? Yes—but cortisol is also responsible for storage of visceral fat, the dangerous stuff that our body tucks deep inside our tummy. For our weight-loss purposes, the more we stress, the more we hold onto weight. The more we hold onto weight, the more we stress out. It's a bit of a vicious cycle.

WHAT CAN WE DO TO IMPROVE?

Be kind to yourself. We don't afford ourselves the same courtesy we offer our friends and family. We look at them with love and respect, while our eyes are often filled with self-loathing and despair when we look at ourselves.

Laws of attraction/mind over matter. Working to keep your mind in the right place is a biggie. The world is truly a different place depending on your own outlook; is the glass half-empty, instead of being half-full? The grass IS always greener on the other side of the fence...UNLESS you focus hard on watering your own grass. Look for that silver lining, put your best foot first and don't let that water glass get to the half-full mark. That glass IS refillable and it's on you to keep it topped up.

Positive energy attracts positive energy. The more you laugh and smile, the more you invite smiling and laughing into your life. Sure, things will still go wrong.

But learning to look at the sunny side of life means an easier recovery after you fall. Every. Single. Time.

Regular exercise. Exercise is not necessary to lose weight. If you're eating a well-balanced ketogenic diet, you will lose weight. While you can't out-exercise a bad diet, our bodies were meant to MOVE! Keeping the joints moving is good for your body. Exercise not only tones your body, it's also a great stress relief.

Whether you bat a few balls, toss the pigskin around, or bust a few yoga moves, it's not only good for the body, it's also good for the soul. Exercise releases endorphins (happy chemicals) in your body, relieves anxiety, and also can help to boost your self-confidence. It's win-win!

Laugh. Laughter really is the best medicine. We could learn from children here. Studies show that happy children laugh up to 400 times a day, while adults laugh as low as 15 times daily. Laughter not only signals your body that you're having a good time, it lowers the amount of stress hormones in your body. It connects us with others and helps to improve social interactions. Using the same laws of attraction, the more we laugh, the more we attract laughter and therefore, happy people.

Relaxation techniques. Yoga is not only good for the body; it's also good for the mind. Learning to quiet your mind and harness your own mental power is huge in the world of health. Learn to compartmentalize and place your troubles in a mental box. Focus on love. Focus on joy. Focus on positive attitude, gratitude, passion, and life. Your emotions during this time are so important.

Only allow yourself a limited window to deal with internal worries, a sort of scheduled appointment with yourself, where you allow yourself time to fret.

OTHER TIMES, WORK ON POSITIVE AFFIRMATIONS:

- ✓ I am worthy.
- ✓ I am in control of the mental atmosphere I create. Thoughts can be changed and the positive thoughts I choose are helping me heal.
- ✓ I am a friend to my body. I forgive my body and treat it with the same loving kindness I would like to receive.
- ✓ I am doing everything I can to help my body be well as quickly as possible.

Positive Mantra Repeat after me: I am good enough. Now stand in front of the mirror and say it again: I AM good enough. Do it everyday. I know it feels silly, but it's a part of building self love you ARE good enough and you ARE worth it!

Social gatherings. Surround yourself with positive people, who will lift you up, empower you and leave you with good happy feelings. Drama and turmoil are real suckers of energy and positivity, and it's so important to protect your mental well-being.

Never sit down at a table where you will be the topic of conversation when you get up.

Demand respect. Lastly, get used to demanding respect for yourself—not only while at those special gatherings, but also in your own head. Far too often we convince ourselves that we don't deserve happiness or success, when in fact the opposite is true. Yes, we deserve good things. Yes, we deserve the best.

Don't take your 'self' for granted. While you're working on improving the physical aspects through ketogenics, take the time to work on your outlook and mental stance. Every step you can take towards great mental health is a great thing for you!

CARBING UP

There is chatter about the need for resetting our normal internal keto settings. The human body is incredibly good at adapting to change; at some point, will our keto body start looking at fat as 'same old, same old', and hunker itself down into the comfortable rut that it was in while we were carb-fueled? Could that be why some people see a stall on the scales?

Would resetting our keto cause us to see bigger losses on the scale? Would carbing up jump-start us to a new level? We sacrificed ourselves for the sake of science and decided to test this theory. We got the nod from our family doctor and off we went.

We chose carefully. We wanted to test the theory, but didn't want chemicals and uglies in our bellies that would cause more complications than the extra carbs would themselves. We chose a restaurant, and also decided to use a friendly carb that we both loved and thoroughly enjoyed in our previous life. If we were going to do this, we might as well consume something we liked, right? (We don't want to trigger others, so our method of carbing up will remain nameless.)

We placed our order. I have to admit, there was some anticipation, sitting and waiting for that old comfort meal. I was excited to taste the old faithful, but I was scared as well. I had heard so many others telling tales of the after-effects of carbing up. Was I going to get sick? Was I going to have to rush to the bathroom?

The first thing I noticed when our food arrived was the complete and utter lack of taste. What we once considered yummy was now like eating a plateful of cardboard. Every single component of the dish was flat and tasteless.

Second observation was the bloat. I had arrived at the restaurant, skivvering my pants up around my waist as I walked in the door, because they were too big. After the meal there was a dead weight in my stomach, and my pants were so tight that I had to undo the top button.

We didn't have to wait for long after that....

Nausea and stomach ache. Upset tummy, more bloat and yes, very fast trips to the bathroom. The fears that I had worried about all came true. It was almost as if our stomachs shut down and downright refused to process this food. The very worst part was that the only movement on the scales was the negative kind.

I did eventually lose the pounds that our carb-up made me gain, and the bloat eventually went away. As I was experiencing it all, at least dear Sidekick was going though the exact same thing right alongside me. Lesson learned, and the carb-up was debunked.

S **In our opinion, carb-ups are not recommended. Make sure you have two separate bathrooms if you do try this experiment at home. Never trust a keto fart.**

TAKING KETO ON THE ROAD

There are many restaurants popping up that cater to the keto culture, but for the most part it's up to you to get your dietary needs addressed. Eating out can be a challenge for ketonians; it's hard to know what to eat in your own kitchen, but eating out opens up so many wild cards. Grilled meats can be covered in a sweet sauce, scrambled eggs can have pancake batter added, salad dressings can be full of canola oil and sugars.

LEARN TO DEFINE YOUR KETO

The single biggest piece of advice I can give you is to learn how to define your keto. The word keto means different things to different people. If you only tell a server that you're keto, they might be basing their recommendation off the last customer who ate what they wanted, but then ate a 'keto pill'. That's not real keto! Here's how I would define my keto: I tell the server that I don't eat grains, potatoes, rice, soy, starches, and sugars, and I try my best to avoid additives, preservatives and veggie oils.

Staying in ketosis while away from home is doable! If you lay the proper groundwork, you can get through a meal, or even an extended holiday, and stay in ketosis.

Here are some tips that can help you stay on track.

Travelling. Planning ahead is key. If travelling by plane, have your agent contact the airline in advance to explain your dietary needs. They may not have an official keto meal, but knowing about your keto way of eating (WOE) in advance may bring you closer to getting keto-approved foods for you to eat.

tip **Don't order the diabetic meal on a plane! It's 99% carbs!**

Purchase freezer packs and a small cooler bag that folds up for easy storage. Food items like nuts, dried meats, boiled eggs, prepared veggies, pork rinds, seaweed chips, and dark chocolate can be kept on ice and will help keep 'the hangrys' away. Pre-scheduled intermittent fasting can help when bringing keto food with you is not an option. Get yourself in the 'I'm choosing not to eat' state of mind, and mentally opt out instead of stressing over what you can eat. When traveling by car, be strategic with your stops. Most gas stations will not have a great food selection for ketonians; steer clear of the snack aisles.

Hotel. Request a mini bar or even a kitchenette at your hotel to keep a stash of keto-approved foods and snacks. Don't let jet lag or a long day driving in the car throw you off your keto plan. Be smart and rest up! Take time to find the local grocery shops in your area, and stock up on pre-cooked bacon, pre-cooked chicken, olives, cans of tuna, ham, or chicken that can easily get you through your day. Ask hotel staff for recommendations. They're the experts in their area and may have insight to help you find things to make your stay successful. Purchase some keto-approved whipping cream to keep in the hotel mini fridge. A small plastic container from home can be washed daily to take out travelling, providing you with the creamy fix for your coffee. Locate food markets and food trucks; they are usually well-oiled and compact restaurants. They are passionate about their food and know their menu inside and out. Stocking up on a hotel breakfast of bacon, sausage, and eggs before you head out for your day can keep you from making bad spur-of-the-moment decisions.

PACK LIST – ITEMS TO TAKE FROM HOME:

- ✓ Cooler bag
- ✓ Sweetener
- ✓ Small container (for coffee cream e.g.)
- ✓ Pork Rinds
- ✓ Boiled eggs
- ✓ Cheeses
- ✓ Cans of tuna, chicken, ham
- ✓ Keto-approved whipping cream
- ✓ Deli meats
- ✓ Pickles
- ✓ A plan for intermittent fasting (see note in 'Breaking Your Fast')

Restaurants. Ask questions! Any restaurant can be keto as long as you ask the right questions! Is there any breading on this? What oils are used here? Does the chef use starches? As long as you're polite and kind, most servers are great at assisting in times like this. Remember, if it's not made in the restaurant and they don't know the ingredients, chances are it's from a can. Avoid!!

> Start your homework before you go. Most restaurants have online menus, so check them before you leave home.

Explain your keto to your server as soon as possible, as this will allow them time to confer with their kitchen team. They might rise to the occasion and add a keto-friendly item to their standard menu. Always be kind, patient and respectful; these are mostly honest and hard-working folks, and they can either make or break your meal out.

Choose grilled meat and vegetables whenever possible. Make sure to ask if the meat was marinated or brined in sugar or honey. If this is the case, you can request one that hasn't been pre-soaked.

Green salads are usually a safe option, but ask about dressing or sauce ingredients. Most restaurants will help you with a basic oil vinaigrette in place of sugary commercial dressings. Always request sauces and condiments on the side.

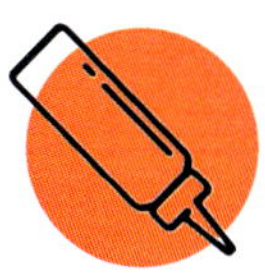

Condiments can make or break a meal! There are good and bad versions of every sauce and condiment. Always check ingredients and practise due diligence.

KETO-'CAN' CONDIMENTS:

✓ **Hot sauce, mustard, olive oils, béchamel, hollandaise, salsa, dill relish, nut butters, broth or bouillon, pesto, horseradish.**

KETO-'CAN NOT' CONDIMENTS:

✗ **Ketchup, BBQ sauce, honey, hummus, soy, tamari, plum sauce, tartar, teriyaki, sweet relish, chili and cocktail sauce.**

Eggs are always a great option. Many restaurants offer a 24-hour breakfast, so why not go for breakfast for dinner? Omelettes or a Western sandwich (skip the bread, of course) are also great options, but ask to make sure they don't put additives like pancake batter in their eggs. A big plate of bacon with a side salad is always an option. Most restaurants will accommodate you with naked burgers or burgers in a lettuce wrap. You don't need to bail on dessert, either. Ask for a small bowl of berries and whipping cream for a quick sweet treat, or finish with a cheese plate.

KETOING THE CUISINES

Sushi Sashimi primarily consists of fresh and raw seafood and is often a safe choice.

Vietnamese Choose pho or ramen without noodles.

Mexican Fajitas without the tortillas are a great choice. Just use your fork and knife, or ask for lettuce cups. Ask for salsa, onion, guacamole, lettuce, tomatoes, peppers, and sour cream on the side. Other options include chili verde, a burrito bowl (without the burrito), or ceviche. Don't forget avocado!

Italian Steak, chicken, pork, or fish are great options here. Ask about the meatball and marinara ingredients; if they're clean they can be a good indulgent meal. Many restaurants are doing spiralized veggies and crustless pizzas using a cheese base, so it never hurts to ask. Choose dark leafy greens, olive oil, Parmesan cheese, and crushed garlic. Alfredo can be a good option here, as is Caesar salad with no croutons.

Pub/ Sports Grill Naked wings, steaks, grilled chicken, pork chops (with no breading), grilled salmon, burger without the bun, or a Caesar salad with no croutons are all good choices.

Burger/ BBQ Joint Beware of dipping sauces and non-keto condiments. Bunless burgers, lettuce cups, grilled meats, Caesar salad with no croutons, or wings with salad on the side are possible choices. Inquire about ingredients.

French French restaurants are often great choices for keto meals. Try something like Chicken Provençal, duck confit, steak tartare, charcuterie, Coq au Vin, or Beef Bourguignon. Inquire about ingredients.

Asian Watch the ingredients here, there are sugars and sauces galore! Instead, opt for grilled meats, seafood, and veggies. Possible choices include plain roasted duck meat, ribs, meat soups, or stir-fries, but make sure there's no added sugar in the sauce. Hot and sour soup, egg drop soup, or chicken broth with scallions are good options.

Greek Try skewers, gyros, meatballs, and kebabs with veggies on the side. Inquire about the ingredients and have sauces on the side.

Indian Coconut-based curries and roasted meats, as well as some butter chicken recipes, are good keto choices. Inquire about sauce ingredients and ask for them on the side. Possible choices include Tandoori chicken/shrimp/lamb without naan bread or rice, roasted eggplant, meat tikka (very similar to tandoori) or chicken korma.

Any time you're taking keto on the road, be mindful of these things:

Choose your meal mates wisely. It can be challenging to keto on if your table-mate is not supportive of your way of eating.

Stay away from that slippery slope of carbs. Having a small bite or two can lead you through the gateway of waking carb cravings and derailed keto. Cheating will make you feel bloated and lead to stomach upset. Nobody wants that while on holidays.

Worse case scenario, if you accidentally eat more carbs than you should, stay the course! Especially if you're fat-adapted; it's easy to get back on track.

Beware the beer. Beer is known as liquid bread for a reason; if they don't have a low-carb version, steer clear. Remember that alcohol hits you harder when you're in ketosis, so easy does it.

Protect yourself from known weak spots. Know your strengths and weaknesses and steer clear of those items that create temptation.

Belly up to the water trough. Make sure your water glass is always full while at the table. It will help you feel full and keep you on track.

Search out the fats. Just like at home, add butter, oils, and cream. Beware of vegetable oil, it's super inflammatory and is not keto!

The single most important tip of all, is once you've done your homework and made the best decision that you can, just enjoy your meal.

Most of us ketonian folk don't get to eat out often, so when you do, soak it all up and enjoy the whole experience. Enjoy a great meal and best of all, leave the dishes to somebody else!

To make the most of *East Coast Keto 2*, keep your eyes peeled for these symbols:

Timing Tips

Recipe Pairings & Alternative Ingredients

Tips & Tricks

Sidekick Comments

Listen to Your Body

One of the best things you can do for yourself is to take your eating off the clock! When you eat three meals a day as scheduled by the clock, you're not only training your body to accept food at a certain time of day, you're also shutting down your body's way of telling you when you're naturally hungry/thirsty. Let me explain.

Our body is fueled by food. When you burn energy, your body will need that energy replenished, so it sends a signal that it needs food. When you are warm, or are exerting energy, your body will also need water. When you push past hunger to wait until 'suppertime' you're shutting down a communication pathway in your own body. That same pathway also tells you when you are full. You learn not to listen to that message, and end up eating past fullness, eating more than you need. Let that sink in.

Eat when you're hungry and drink when your body tells you it's thirsty. Simple!

APPETIZERS & SNACKS

Crab-Stuffed Mushrooms | 32

Crab Rangoon | 35

Frikkin' Deadly Chocolate Granola | 36

Miss Bobbi's Snack Chips with Seasoning Blends | 38

Mushroom Risotto | 41

Pig Candy [A Sidekick Recipe] | 42

Ricotta and Tomato Bruschetta | 44

Roasted Crispy Pork Ravioli with Rustic Tomato Sauce | 46

Scotch Eggs | 50

Stuffed Calamari Rings | 53

All macro counts given are per serving.

A simple crowd-pleaser that will delight both guests and family. No sauces necessary.

CRAB-STUFFED MUSHROOMS

SERVINGS 16 **SERVING SIZE** 1 crab-stuffed mushroom

16 large fresh mushrooms

oil, for brushing

4 oz cream cheese, softened

6 oz cooked crab, cooled and minced

2 green onions, thinly sliced

⅓ cup Parmesan cheese, grated

2 tbsp parsley, chopped

½ tsp garlic powder

½ tsp Himalayan pink salt

⅛ tsp pepper

1. Preheat the oven to 375°F.
2. Remove any debris from mushrooms.
3. Using a small spoon or corer, remove stems and spoon out the insides of the mushroom. Set removed pieces aside for later use in another recipe—waste not, want not!
4. Brush mushrooms with oil.
5. Mix cream cheese until smooth. Stir in remaining ingredients.
6. Spoon the filling into the mushroom caps.
7. Place the filled mushrooms on a parchment-covered baking sheet.
8. Bake 18-20 minutes or until cooked through and tops are golden.

carbs	fibre	fat	protein
1.5g	0g	3g	5g

Cheese filling will be super hot! Allow the mushroom caps time to cool before eating.

A rangoon is a fancy name for a Chinese dumpling or wonton. These can be deep fried, baked, or even added to a gently simmering soup. We've used crab in this recipe, but you can easily swap out any protein; chicken, shrimp, lobster, beef, or crab all work well. Or, skip the meat altogether and just go with a cheesy/veggie variation of this filling.

Either way, these Crab Rangoons will be a star on your plate no matter what you put inside as filling. This highly customizable dish is a great one to make your own by adding your own clever little tweaks. Make sure you keep track of your preferred homemade variations!

Ensure all fillings are precooked. Wontons can also be fried in 350°F oil until browned and crispy, roughly 1-2 minutes.

CRAB RANGOON

SERVINGS 12 **SERVING SIZE** 1 dumpling or 1 rangoon

12 wonton wrappers, approximately 3 inches in size and rolled out thin (see recipe page 213)

FOR THE FILLING

8 oz cooked crab, cooled and minced

8 oz cream cheese

1 egg

1 large clove garlic, minced

1 tsp green onion or chives

1 tsp dehydrated onion

¼ tsp fish sauce

oil, for brushing

1. Preheat oven to 325°F.
2. Mix all filling ingredients together.
3. Add 1 tsp of filling to the centre of the wrapper.
4. Using your fingers or a pastry brush, slightly dampen the edges of a wrapper with water to make them sticky, then fold the wonton in half and fold over the edge on top of itself, creating a seal. Or if you prefer, bundle the pastry at the top to form a sack, similar to a potsticker or dumpling. Either way, ensure they are well-sealed and all air has been squeezed out of the parcels.
5. Run a damp finger all along the outside edge of the joined pastry and let sit for a few minutes. This extra step ensures a good seal on the edge.
6. Brush a layer of keto-friendly oil over the outside of the pastry. We used bacon fat.
7. Bake in the oven for about 10 minutes, or until the rangoon is golden brown.
8. Let cool slightly—the cheese will be molten hot—and serve with your favourite dipping sauce. Our favourite is hoisin (see our recipe on page 193.)

note The macros for this recipe include both the filing and wrappers.

carbs	fibre	fat	protein
5.3g	2.4g	14g	10g

There's no other way to describe this granola; it's just frikkin' deadly. This keto-friendly granola can either be crumbled up into smaller pieces, as a cereal with whipping cream or almond milk, or left as a snack in the form of bite-size pieces. We keep this on hand to add to our charcuterie boards. It provides an extra little sweet to end off an awesome snack. Omit the chocolate if you want a plain granola.

FRIKKIN' DEADLY CHOCOLATE GRANOLA

SERVINGS 12 **SERVING SIZE** ½ cup

- 1 cup almonds, sliced
- 1 cup pecans, chopped
- 1 cup unsweetened coconut, shaved or coarsely shredded
- 1 large egg, whisked
- ½ cup pumpkin seeds
- ½ cup sunflower seeds
- ½ cup flax seed or meal
- ½ cup hemp seeds
- ½ cup butter, melted
- ½ cup powdered sweetener
- 2 tsp vanilla or maple extract
- ½ tsp salt
- ½ cup Baker's chocolate, shaved or chopped (optional)

1. Preheat the oven to 300°F and line a baking sheet with parchment paper.
2. Add all ingredients to a medium-size mixing bowl and stir to combine.
3. Spoon the granola onto the baking sheet.
4. Bake for 10 minutes, then remove and stir the granola.
5. Bake for another 10 minutes for a softer granola, or another 20-25 minutes for crispy granola. Don't let it burn!
6. Remove granola from the oven and let cool. Granola will crisp up as it cools.
7. Transfer to refrigerator; chill uncovered overnight or for 12 hours.
8. Enjoy!

carbs	fibre	fat	protein
13.3g	8.6g	41g	15g

Store this granola in snack-sized bags, inside a freezer bag, in the freezer.

Omit Baker's chocolate for a plain granola. If you want chocolate chips instead of an all-chocolate granola, add them to the mix after you remove the granola from the oven and it has slightly cooled. Stir them in and then let sit to cool completely.

I think we've gone and done it! We've gone and created the perfect keto faux-tato snack chip, and we're so happy about it! We're all missing a bag of chips, aren't we? That crispness and that salty flavour? C'mon! Sure, ya knows you are! These keto-friendly snacks will have the crunch of kettle chips and the true clean flavours of keto living.

MISS BOBBI'S SNACK CHIP [WITH SEASONING BLENDS]

1 medium-size celeriac (celery root)

keto-friendly oil, for frying

1. Peel celeriac, making certain to carefully dig out any cracks and crevices that could have soil or dirt.
2. Using a mandolin and a guard, carefully slice the celeriac into very thin pieces. We use the smallest setting on our mandolin.
3. Deep-fry the chips at 350°F for about 10 minutes, or until the chips are golden brown, edging towards brown.

note **These chips must be crispy!**

4. Remove from oil and place in a medium-size bowl. Toss with your favourite chip seasoning.

SEASONING BLENDS

Here, we've provided a smattering of seasonings to try.
You can go right to your fave (mine's ketchup), or have fun trying them all!

PLAIN GARLIC

- 1 tsp salt
- 1 tsp garlic powder
- ½ tsp pepper

KETCHUP

- 1 tsp smoked paprika (or regular paprika)
- ½ tsp salt
- ½ tsp onion powder
- ½ tsp garlic powder

ALL-DRESSED

- 2 tsp chili powder
- 2 tsp smoked paprika
- 1 tsp dry mustard powder
- 1 tsp cumin
- 1 tsp garlic powder
- 1 tsp onion powder
- ½ tsp cayenne

ROAST CHICKEN

- 1 tsp turmeric
- ½ tsp thyme
- ½ tsp salt

BBQ

- 1 tsp onion powder
- 1 tsp smoked paprika
- 1 tsp powdered sweetener
- 1 tsp fine sea or Himalayan pink salt
- 1 tsp chili powder
- 1 tsp garlic powder
- ½ tsp ground ginger
- ½ tsp black pepper

DILL

- 1 tsp dill
- 1 tsp garlic powder
- 1 tsp salt
- ½ tsp onion powder
- ½ tsp Korean chili flakes

CACCIATORE SPICE

- 1 tsp smoked paprika
- 1 tsp onion powder
- 1 tsp oregano
- 1 tsp ground fennel
- 1 tsp salt

CHEESE

- 1 tsp nutritional yeast
- 1 tsp garlic powder
- 1 pinch chili powder
- ¼ tsp salt
- ¼ tsp black pepper

SALT AND VINEGAR

- 2 tbsp sea salt
- 2 tbsp pickling vinegar

Mix all ingredients together in a wide bottomed bowl; we used a pie plate.

Allow to dry at room temperature, or dry in your dehydrator or oven on the lowest temperature until the salt has returned to its granular form and is not moist at all.

We smash our seasoning mixes with a mortar and pestle to make sure herbs, seeds and other ingredients are powdered and consolidated.

SERVINGS/MACROS

Celeriac can vary in size from 7 ounces to over 2 pounds! Because of the variance in size of this veggie and the fact that each one will need a portion of the root removed, we recommend you work out your own macros for this recipe based on the size of your chosen celeriac and how much you consume.

Many foodies would argue that a true risotto needs at least 20 minutes for the rice dish to come together. Since we're using a konjac rice that's already at the right consistency, the timeline is not as important. In this case, it's all about 'the finish' and making sure the end product is creamy and full of that mushroom/umami flavour.

We're totally fine with the fact that that the traditional foodies might wrinkle their noses at our risotto; we just hope you and your family fall in love with it.

MUSHROOM RISOTTO

SERVINGS 8 **SERVING SIZE** ½ cup

1. Remove konjac rice from the package. Drain, rinse well, dry with paper towel, then set aside.
2. Heat oil in a large sauté pan over medium-high heat. Stir in the mushrooms, and cook until mushrooms are soft and slightly brown, about 3 minutes. Remove mushrooms and set aside.
3. Add the onion to the pan. Cook 2-3 minutes, then add garlic.
4. Stir in konjac rice and cook about 2-3 minutes, then pour in wine and broth, stirring constantly.
5. Cook until the liquid has absorbed.
6. Reduce heat and add cream, salt, and pepper. Continue to cook and stir until the cream has been absorbed.
7. Remove from heat, and stir in mushrooms (reserve a few for garnish), butter, chives, and parmesan. Check salt and pepper and adjust to taste.
8. Stir thoroughly until the ingredients are well-mixed and the texture is thick and creamy.
9. Serve with a handful of freshly grated Parmesan and chives.

- 1 package konjac rice
- 2 tbsp olive oil
- 1 lb portobello or baby Bella mushrooms, thinly sliced
- 1 medium onion, diced
- 3 cloves garlic, minced
- ½ cup dry white wine
- ⅔ cup chicken or veggie broth
- ¼ cup 35% whipping cream
- sea salt, to taste
- pinch pepper, to taste
- 4 tbsp butter
- 3 tbsp chives, finely chopped
- ½ cup Parmesan cheese, freshly grated

carbs	fibre	fat	protein
8.9g	3.4g	14g	14g

sidekick recipe

Pork belly is a meat that a lot of ketonians use as a staple ingredient. Really, this is just the uncured cut from the underbelly of the pig—the bacon cut. Sure, it tastes just as good as regular old bacon, but we can help you to take this incredible cut of meat and turn it into something so fantastic, it's just like candy—Pig Candy, that is.

This is a very simple dish and if done properly, it is the most decadent protein combined with a wonderful bang of flavour from seasoning and fat content. Make sure you use a deep pan while roasting these to catch all the drippings; you'll want to save it as a free source of fat to keep next to your stove.

This recipe is downright delicious when it's warm, chewy, crispy, and straight from the oven/grill, but our favourite is the leftover bits that we store in the fridge in a zip-lock bag. Cold crunchy pig candy! Make sure to save yourself some to try this way! This is another of these low and slow cooks that will be well worth the wait.

PIG CANDY

SERVINGS 16 **SERVING SIZE** 2oz

- 2 lb pork belly slab
- 1 cup BBQ Sauce—see recipes on page 190
- salt and pepper to taste
- apple cider vinegar for spraying

note Nutrition does not include BBQ sauce; please add in the macros for the sauce that you use for your pig candy.

carbs	fibre	fat	protein
0g	0g	30g	5.5g

1. Preheat oven to 250 °F.
2. Cut the pork into 1-inch square pieces that are the full thickness of the slab.
3. Season all over with salt and pepper. Don't skimp on the salt here; salt allows the meat to retain moisture as it cooks.
4. Place the pork pieces on a grate or rack over a pan to catch drippings. Making sure to keep a little space between each piece. We want these to crisp up, and overcrowding the pan will prevent that from happening.
5. Roast for 2 hours or until meat is starting to cook/reduce in size and fat has started to render. Don't flip before you see this. Cook time will vary depending on the thickness of the meat and the temperature of your oven. Spritz every hour with apple cider vinegar.
6. Remove from the oven and turn the pieces over, then return to the oven for another 2 hours.
7. Drain and reserve the fat from the bottom of the pan. Remove the racks at this time, placing the pieces directly into the pan.

   note Pieces should be crispy on the outside, with most of the fat rendered at this point. If not, put them back in the oven again for more time without sauce.

8. Once in the pan, add your chosen sauce and toss to coat on all sides.
9. Return to the oven for another 1 ½ to 2 hours, saucing and tossing again about halfway through.
10. Continue cooking until the sauce has caramelized over the pork.
11. Remove from the oven and enjoy.

FOR THE SMOKER use a slightly lower temperature of 225°F and smoke for 6-7 hours. Spritz every hour with apple cider vinegar. This helps to keep the meat tender.

FOR THE GRILL use your BBQ as an oven. Turn on one burner and close your lid. Wait for the temperature to stabilize and then regulate the temperature by lowering or raising your burner to the desired temp. When you find that sweet spot, place your meat in the BBQ on the opposite side from the lit burner (indirect heat) and close the grill. Your BBQ is now an oven! Once you have your grill temperature stabilized, return to instructions for oven method.

We make extra of this recipe so we can have cold leftover pig candy the next day. Store them in a freezer-type bag for a grab-and-go keto-friendly treat.

RICOTTA AND TOMATO BRUSCHETTA

This keto-friendly bruschetta is dressed up with ricotta and herb salad. It's a perfect snack for company, or for a quick snack when you have some leftover pizza crust or keto bread kicking around the house.

Try it—we're sure you're gonna love it!

SERVINGS 4 **SERVING SIZE** 1 slice

FOR THE TOPPING

1 cup ricotta

1 tsp thyme

1 tsp dried basil

1 tsp oregano

1 tsp salt, or to taste

½ tsp chili flakes

¼ cup olive oil

¼ tsp pepper

FOR THE BASE

1 garlic clove, pulverized and salted—we use a mortar and pestle

2 tbsp butter, room temperature

4 slices keto bread—use any, but we prefer our Tastes Like Real Bread Keto Bread from our first book (page 249)

TO FINISH

½ cup baby heirloom tomatoes, halved and salted

1 cup, any combination of fresh basil, parsley, tarragon, dill, or oregano, chopped

olive oil to drizzle

salt and cracked pepper to taste

1. Whip all topping ingredients together with a whisk or spoon. Set aside.
2. Combine garlic with butter and spread on the bread. Toast in a toaster oven or regular oven for about 10 minutes or until the toast is golden brown.
3. Divide topping mix into 4 servings and spread it on top of your toast.
4. Place the salted tomatoes on top and sprinkle the herb mix over the tomatoes.
5. Drizzle oil over the top.
6. Finish with salt and pepper to taste.

carbs	fibre	fat	protein
4.25g	0.5g	15g	8g

note Nutrition does not include bread. That will depend on what keto bread you use.

These crispy little bundles of lusciousness make a perfect appetizer to warm up your guest's bellies, or you can pair it with a Caesar salad for a full-size meal.

Our preference is to pile these up in a serving bowl alongside a bowl of the sauce. Individual appetizer plates or even cocktail napkins will do in a pinch to make this a hands-on, delicious activity.

For a vegetarian option, replace meat with sautéed spinach. Any tomatoes can be used, but we prefer the San Marzanos because they are richer in taste. Nutrition does not include the wrapper macros.

ROASTED CRISPY PORK RAVIOLI *with* RUSTIC TOMATO SAUCE

SERVINGS 16 **SERVING SIZE** ½ cup

FOR THE SAUCE

- 2 tbsp oil
- 1 medium onion, chopped
- ½ cup mushroom, rough chopped
- ½ cup pepper, rough chopped
- 2 tsp oregano
- 1 tsp basil
- ½ thyme
- ½ tsp rosemary
- ¼ tsp nutmeg
- ¼ cup apple cider vinegar
- 1 can (28 oz) San Marzano tomatoes, rough chopped

SAUCE

carbs	fibre	fat	protein
3.4g	1g	2g	0.75g

FOR THE SAUCE

1. Add oil to a sauté pan preheated over medium heat.
2. Add onion and cook until they start to turn translucent, about 5 minutes.
3. Add mushrooms, peppers, and spices and cook for another 5 minutes.
4. Use the vinegar to deglaze the pan and get all the tasty bits off the bottom of the pan. Cook for at least 5 minutes to allow the vinegar to mellow. Add ¼ cup of water if the pan gets too dry.
5. Add the tomatoes and stir to combine. Continue to heat for another 5 minutes, then turn off the heat. The tomatoes need to stay chunky here; if they cook for too long, they will dissolve into the sauce.
6. Set sauce aside until you're ready to plate the dish.

FOR THE RAVIOLI

1. Add oil to a large sauté pan over medium heat.
2. Add pork and onion and cook for about 5 minutes.
3. Add garlic, Parmesan cheese and spices to the pan and continue to cook for 3 to 5 minutes.

4. Use the apple cider vinegar to deglaze and get those crispy tasty bits off the bottom of the pan.
5. Remove meat mix from the heat and place in the refrigerator to chill for at least half an hour.
6. When the filling is fully cooled, place it in the food processor along with the cottage cheese.
7. Pulse the mix until it reaches a paté consistency. Place in fridge to chill.
8. Make the wrapper dough as outlined on page 213 and place in fridge to chill.
9. When dough has chilled completely, remove it and the filling from fridge.
10. Roll the dough out between two sheets of parchment paper to the desired thickness, and use a round cutter, a pastry cutter, or a pastry roller to make your desired shape.
11. Scoop about a teaspoon of the filling and place it slightly off-centre on the wrapper.
12. Using your finger or a pastry brush, wet the outer edge of the wrapper with water and then fold it in half, encapsulating the filling. As you close the wrapper, ensure all air has been removed from the ravioli.
13. Set aside and continue making ravioli until the wraps are all filled.

note **By this time the ravioli edges will have slightly puffed up and should have totally sealed. Recheck all for any spots that aren't closed completely and brush water on any unsealed areas.**

14. Preheat oven to 350°F.
15. Prepare a baking sheet with a layer of parchment paper.
16. Brush a thin layer of oil on each of the filled pasta and arrange them, evenly spaced, on the cookie sheet.
17. Bake for 7-8 minutes, or until the pastry is golden brown and the filling is heated through.
18. Let cool slightly.
19. Warm rustic sauce (if needed) and spoon up into individual side bowls.
20. Stack the crispy ravioli in a large serving bowl and place family-style in the centre of your table with a bowl of the rustic sauce at each place setting.

FOR THE RAVIOLI

- 1 batch of our wraps (See 'Wontons and Fine Pastry, page 213)
- 1 tbsp oil
- ½ lb pork, minced
- ¼ cup onion, minced
- 1 clove garlic, minced
- ⅓ cup Parmesan cheese
- ¾ tsp oregano
- ¼ tsp basil
- 1 tsp Himalayan pink salt
- ½ tsp pepper
- pinch nutmeg
- 2 tbsp apple cider vinegar, to deglaze
- 1 cup cottage cheese
- ⅛ cup oil, for brushing
- ¼ cup water in a bowl for sealing edges

RAVIOLI

carbs	fibre	fat	protein
1g	0.1g	7g	5g

ROASTED CRISPY PORK RAVIOLI *with* RUSTIC TOMATO SAUCE

Knowing this recipe is even better than knowing the Cadbury Caramilk secret! How to get that crispy crunchy coating, soft sausage middle, and the perfectly cooked runny egg all in one delightful ball of flavour? Pure magic!

There are a couple of secrets to getting these perfect. The first is to be very strict on how long to boil the eggs, and then to put them in ice water right away.

The second is to make a paste as you go between the first two bowls of coating, by rubbing the coated egg gently with your fingers. If you don't do this, the crust will just crumble off the egg when you take it out of the fryer.

SCOTCH EGGS

SERVINGS 6 **SERVING SIZE** 1 egg

- 7 medium eggs, reserving one for the egg wash
- ½ lb sausage meat—see recipe on page 223 in our first book
- 3 tbsp Dijon mustard
- ½ cup coconut flour, for dredging
- ¼ cup water
- ¼ cup flax meal, for dredging
- Himalayan pink salt, and pepper to taste

carbs	fibre	fat	protein
7.5g	4.5g	21g	15g

1. Cover 6 eggs with cold water. Reserve 1 uncooked egg for the egg wash.
2. Heat until water begins to boil. Cover with lid and immediately remove from the heat. Let stand for 3 minutes only.
3. After the 3 minutes, cover eggs with cold water to stop them from cooking. Let stand for 5-10 minutes.
4. Peel eggs using a teaspoon, then set aside.

   note **To peel the eggs, gently remove the shell on the narrow end of the egg just enough to clear away the full top of the egg. Then gently slide a teaspoon in between the egg and the shell, and slide it all the way around the egg.**

5. Combine sausage meat and mustard.
6. Separate sausage mixture into 6 balls.
7. Flatten each meatball and add an egg to the centre.
8. Using your hands, gently wrap sausage meat around the entire egg.
9. Wrap each meat-covered egg in plastic wrap and refrigerate for 10 minutes.

10. Lay out three bowls: one with coconut flour, one with the uncooked egg whisked together with water, and one with flax meal.
11. Season each bowl with salt and pepper. We use ½ tsp salt and ¼ tsp of pepper in each.
12. Roll eggs in the coconut flour to coat, then dip the scotch egg into the bowl with beaten egg.
13. Gently rub the egg wash into the coconut on the Scotch egg ball so that they form a paste. Then dip the paste-covered egg into the flax meal in the third bowl.
14. Refrigerate for 10 minutes.
15. Remove from the fridge and deep fry at 350°F for 2-3 minutes, depending on the size of your egg or until golden brown.
16. Transfer to a cooling rack.
17. Finish in a 375°F oven for 15 minutes.

If you don't like a runny egg, leave the egg in the boiled water for extra increments of 30 seconds, until you get your preferred level of doneness.

Isn't it amazing how your taste changes when you are living a ketogenic lifestyle? Calamari is definitely one of those foods for me. If you had told me years ago that I would be making squid rings for myself to eat, I honestly would have laughed in your face. Yet here I am, the present-day me not only writing a calamari recipe, but also enjoying them. For reals!

You can use a full squid here, but we like the way the individual baked pieces crisp up on both sides of the rings. You can't achieve that by baking the full squid and then cutting it. Hope your family loves this recipe as much as we do!

STUFFED CALAMARI RINGS

SERVINGS 8 **SERVING SIZE** 2 oz

1 lb squid rings, fresh or frozen

FOR THE DRESSING

Two-Minute Bread—see recipe in our first book (page 250). You can also use any keto-friendly bread.

¼ onion, minced

2 tbsp butter, melted

2 tbsp water

Newfoundland (summer) savoury or thyme, to taste

salt and pepper, to taste

oil, for brushing

1. Make Two-Minute Bread and let cool slightly. Dice loaf into small pieces, no bigger than ¼ inch at most.
2. Place onion, butter, and water in a microwave-safe dish and cook for a minute or until onions are translucent. Set aside to cool.
3. Add savoury, salt, and pepper to the diced pieces of bread in a medium-size bowl. Toss to combine.
4. Add slightly cooled butter/onion mix to the crumb mix and combine with your hands, making sure to press the butter into all the crumb.

   note **This dressing should be fairly moist and not dry. Add a little extra butter if the dressing is still on the dry side. The butter will also help with browning.**

5. Preheat oven to 400°F. Line two baking sheets with parchment paper.
6. Rinse and pat dry squid rings. If using frozen squid rings, completely defrost and pat dry. Brush with oil and then season with salt and pepper. Lay rings out flat on your parchment-lined sheet.
7. Fill rings with dressing until the rings are full and the dressing is even across the top of the ring.
8. Bake for about 15-20 minutes until dressing turns a golden brown. Flip rings over and bake an additional 10 minutes, or until both sides are golden brown.
9. Serve with a sprinkle of your favourite vinegar over the top.

note **Nutrition does not include bread. That will depend on what keto bread you use.**

carbs	fibre	fat	protein
5.4g	0g	6.5g	6g

Breaking Your Fast

Many people don't realize it, but you fast every night when you go to sleep. Your body will use up any food reserves pretty quickly, and then your body goes into a natural fasting state as you sleep. This is why the morning meal is breakfast, or breaking the fast.

Intermittent Fasting (IF) is an eating pattern that extends the fasting period between windows of eating. While anyone can fast (IF), we recommend this as an advanced tool to be saved for when you're soundly fat-adapted and your body has had ample time to heal. If you try fasting before this time, you're risking the chance of sending mixed messages to your body and making it think you're just not taking care of yourself again. Heal your metabolism first and wait 'til you're soundly fat-adapted. As a bonus, if you wait 'til you are fat-adapted, your body won't get hungry in the same way as before, so fasting will be a breeze.

For IF, we recommend using the ideal fasting windows of between 18 and 24 hours. This is when maximum autophagy occurs. Our cells become old and worn out. Autophagy allows our cells to regenerate, as some of the old parts are replaced with souped-up brand-new parts (cells.) So, fasting is somewhat of a reversal of the aging process; it gets rid of old body cells and replaces them with new ones.

Autophagy is the body's way of cleaning out damaged cells, in order to regenerate newer, healthier cells. It is an evolutionary self-preservation mechanism through which the body can remove the dysfunctional cells and recycle parts of them toward cellular repair and cleaning. We often use the car analogy to explain autophagy: imagine you own an older car; it looks great on the outside, but when you pop the hood you see the truth! The wiring has rusted, the electronics are old and tired. But imagine if you replaced that wiring harness and swapped in brand-new electronics—wouldn't that give that old clunker a new lease on life? Autophagy works the same way for our bodies.

BREAKFAST & BRUNCH

Basic Omelette Recipe | 56

Breakfast Pizza | 59

Corned Beef Meat Cakes | 60

Crêpes with Hazelnut Sauce and Strawberries | 62

Dutch Baby | 64

Eggs Florentine | 67

Farmer's Casserole | 68

Ham and Green Onion Chaffle | 71

Jiggs Dinner Breakfast Croquettes | 72

Keto Hash Browns | 75

Newfoundland Toutons | 76

Peanut Butter 'n' Jelly Pancakes | 78

All macro counts given are per serving.

The basic omelette is something I have seen done time and time again, and even though it looked easy, it was a dish I could never master. They always fell apart as I was flipping them, were messy, or just not pretty to look at. All the taste was there but my omelettes were a visual flop.

The secret, I've learned, is to make sure you cook the fillings in advance, instead of trying to cook them in the pan first and then adding the egg on top. You need to give the egg base time to set properly in the bottom of the pan before adding the fillings. Otherwise, you're just making scrambled eggs with fancy fixings mixed in.

BASIC OMELETTE RECIPE

SERVINGS 2 **SERVING SIZE** ½ an omelette

FOR THE FILLING

1 tbsp bacon fat, or equivalent

2 tbsp ham or alternate meat, diced

2 tbsp bell peppers, diced

1 tbsp green onions, diced

1 tbsp tomatoes, diced and drained on paper towel

1 oz cheddar cheese, grated

FOR THE EGG BASE

3 eggs

salt and pepper, to taste

2 tbsp keto-friendly oil

1. Precook filling items (except for cheese) and set aside to cool.
2. Add eggs, salt, and pepper to a small mixing bowl and whisk thoroughly to combine.
3. Add oil to a non-stick sauté pan over medium-high heat.
4. When pan is hot, add the eggs and immediately start to move the eggs in the pan using a small plastic spatula, creating roads or tunnels in the egg. Keep the eggs moving for a full 30 seconds and then turn heat back down to the lowest setting.
5. Using the spatula, smooth the surface of the egg, ensuring there is full coverage of the bottom of the pan. Also take the time to break up or squish any larger pieces of egg. We're looking for one solid layer of cooked egg.
6. Cover with lid and let sit for about 1 minute.
7. Remove cover and tilt the pan to move any still-liquid egg to one side of the pan. Using the spatula, lift an edge of the omelette to allow any liquid egg to flow into the pan.

carbs	fibre	fat	protein
2g	0.5g	32g	12g

Make sure all fillings are precooked before adding to omelette. You can watch our East Coast Keto YouTube video for an easy tutorial for this recipe.

8. When you're satisfied that most of the liquid egg on top has been moved under (egg still will be moist and shiny) add precooked filling and cheese to one half of the omelette. Turn off heat and cover with lid.
9. After 30 seconds to a minute, depending on thickness, remove lid. All the egg should now be fully cooked from residual and internal heat. If not, re-cover and wait another 30 seconds or so.
10. Use the spatula to gently lift the edge of the omelette on the opposite side of the filling. As you lift the omelette with your small spatula, slip your egg turner into the cavity you have created and flip the omelette in half, over onto itself.
11. Use your egg turner to transfer the omelette from the pan to the plate.

The egg will continue to cook after you have plated it, so be careful not to overcook.

Pizza for breakfast? Why not?! We absolutely adore cold keto pizza for breakfast, but it's also super fun to specially create one, topped with breakfast-type foods for a morning treat. When we make our skinny face pizza crust, we always do a triple batch of the dough and most times, a crust is set aside for breakfast pizza!

Make this recipe your own by changing up the veggies and meats. If your family is picky, try making individual pizzas and turn it into a fun kitchen activity by letting the kids decide on their own personal toppings!

Increase cooking time for a medium or well-done egg.

BREAKFAST PIZZA

SERVINGS 4 **SERVING SIZE** 1 slice

One 9-inch skinny face crust pizza base—recipe found on page 210

1-2 tbsp marinara sauce

SUGGESTED TOPPINGS

1 tomato, sliced

1 large egg

2 strips bacon, cooked and chopped into one-inch sections

½ cup mozzarella cheese, shredded (optional)

Garnish with chiffonade of basil.

To chiffonade the basil, roll fresh basil leaves into a cigar shape then cut into thin slices.

1. Bake skinny face pizza crust.
2. Spoon on marinara sauce and arrange toppings.
3. Add egg to the top and bake for 10 minutes at 350°F, or until white is firm and yolk is still loose.

   Note **Increase cooking time in increments of 30 seconds, if you like your eggs a little firmer.**

4. Sprinkle cheese and basil over the top, if using, after you take the warm pizza out of the oven.

We prefer not to add cheese to the top as the crust is made of cheese; adding more on top often makes the pizza too heavy.

This recipe can be customized to suit your own tastes; more eggs, ham, sausage, mushroom, or different veggies can be switched out or added. You can use any marinara sauce, but we prefer our own recipe, found on page 232 in our first book.

carbs	fibre	fat	protein
3.4g	0.6g	25g	26g

Take caution in picking out your can of corned beef; many of these contain starches. Starches are like super-sugars and should be avoided at all costs. Check ingredients.

We loved these meat cakes as kids! Ours were usually smothered with ketchup, but I remember Mom and Dad having theirs with some sweet mustard pickles over the top.

Just to be adult, when we tested this keto version of the meat cake, we had to try both the ketchup and the pickles. Yet again, Mom and Dad were right. Theses meat cakes are nice with the ketchup, but when you add the pickles (see Sweet Adorable Mustard Pickles recipe, page 202) something magical happens. Try them both ways!

CORNED BEEF MEAT CAKES

SERVINGS 8 **SERVING SIZE** 1 meat cake

- 1½ cups cauliflower rice, finely riced
- olive oil, for frying
- 1 medium onion, minced, or 2 tsp dried onion flakes
- 4 cloves garlic, pulverized and salted
- 1 tsp salt
- ½ tsp pepper
- 2 large eggs
- 1 can bully beef or corned beef
- ½ cup almond flour
- 1 tbsp parsley
- 1 tsp thyme
- 1 tsp Dijon mustard
- 1 tsp fish sauce
- 1 tsp paprika
- ½ tsp Korean pepper flakes (optional)

carbs	fibre	fat	protein
4.6g	2g	13g	9.5g

1. Preheat oven to 275°F.
2. This step is key: boil the cauliflower rice and use paper towels to remove the excess water.

   note **Make certain to squeeze all the water out of the cauliflower for a good consistency. We use a paper towel and also place the paper-towel-covered cauliflower in a clean kitchen towel and wring it out.**
3. Blend cauliflower in a bullet or blender. Set aside.
4. Add the oil and onion in a medium-size frying pan over medium heat and sauté onions until translucent.
5. Add the garlic and cook for an additional 2 minutes.
6. Season with salt and pepper and set aside to cool slightly.
7. Combine all remaining ingredients in a large mixing bowl. Add cauliflower and onion mixture and combine thoroughly.
8. Assemble cakes. Cook for 3-5 minutes on each side until the outsides are golden brown.
9. Transfer pan to the oven and finish in the oven for about 10 minutes.

Don't overfill the pan, and add oil as needed.

You can cut your meat into chunks and stir it into the pre-mixed batter at the end, if you prefer chunks of meat rather than having it fully mashed in. If you prefer a meatier cake, cut the amount of almond flour in half, or increase the meat by ½ cup.

If there ever was a finicky recipe, it's this one. I'll give you a heads-up right now; when you first try these crêpes, be prepared for it not to look perfect, and that's okay. It will still taste fine and it's oh so worth the effort.

There are so many sweet and savoury combinations for this recipe, but we chose to dress these super-thin pancakes the way we first had them as a couple, during a long weekend getaway, a mile or so from the base of the Eiffel tower. The homemade hazelnut spread easily steals the show here, but rest assured you can have the crêpes with just whipping cream and berries, or any other flavour combo that works for you and your family.

The secret to this is a dry pan, and lots and lots of patience.

CRÊPES *with* HAZELNUT SAUCE AND STRAWBERRIES

SERVINGS 4 **SERVING SIZE** 1 crêpe

FOR THE SPREAD

- ¾ cup hazelnuts, toasted and husks removed
- ¼ cup keto-friendly oil
- ¼ cup powdered sweetener
- 2 tbsp cocoa powder
- 1 tsp vanilla extract
- pinch nutmeg
- pinch Himalayan pink salt

FOR THE CRÊPES

- 2 eggs
- ⅓ cup 35% whipping cream
- 2 tbsp coconut flour
- 1 tbsp psyllium husk
- 1 tsp cream of tartar
- ½ tsp baking soda

note The amount of spread to use is dependent on your daily macros and how much you enjoy this spread.

carbs	fibre	fat	protein
9.5g	4.25g	38g	7.5g

FOR THE SPREAD

1. Nuts are baked at 350°F for 10 minutes, then rubbed in a clean tea towel to help remove all the husks.
2. Add all ingredients to a blender or bullet, and grind until smooth and fully incorporated.

   note If the mixture is very thick, add an extra tablespoon of oil.

FOR THE CRÊPES

1. Mix all ingredients together and set batter aside to rest for 20 minutes while you work on slicing berries and finishing your spread.
2. Once the batter has rested, get a frying pan with a lid, or use two frying pans: one good non-stick pan and another larger in size than the first, which will be used for a lid. This will turn our frying pan into a small version of an oven.
3. Turn your burner to high and place the pan on it; wait for about 15-20 seconds for the pan to get super hot. Once it is hot, spoon about 3 tbsp of batter into the dry pan.

If your batter is not spreading well, add another tablespoon or two of whipping cream to the batter.

4. The next step is most often described as a swirl, but I think of it as more of a shiver. Lift the pan off the heat and rotate it to shiver or swirl the batter all over the bottom of the pan. This will help to ensure that the bottom is completely covered. Be careful and remember your burner is still on!
5. Cover the pan with the lid and turn the burner to the lowest setting.
6. Place the covered pan back on the burner, and wait for your home-made oven to dry out the top of your crêpe. I try to avoid peeking for at least 30-45 seconds so as not to release the hot air that's cooking our crêpe. After 45 seconds, I gently swirl or run a spatula around the edge of the pan, lifting the rim of the crêpe. At this point I only lift the crêpe edge and don't try to lift the centre of the crëpe itself.
7. Re-cover, turn off the heat and allow your mini stove-top oven to further dry out the top of the crêpe.
8. Gently and slowly run your spatula under the whole bottom of the crêpe. Flip the crêpe over and press it gently onto the bottom of the still-warm pan, until the opposite side is just starting to turn golden brown. Remove to a plate and repeat the process for 3 more crêpes.
9. Load each crêpe up with a spread of hazelnut, a few berries, or other desired filling, and fold in half or quarters. Bon appétit!

Take care when you're shivering the batter. Your stove burner is on and not covered with a pan. Be mindful!

If your crêpe needs another few seconds on the burner, turn your burner to low heat and cover. Only leave the burner on for about 10 seconds at this point, and let residual heat do the trick.

A Dutch Baby is similar to a large Yorkshire pudding or popover. They are always baked in the oven, are thicker than traditional pancakes, and contain no leavening ingredients such as baking soda. This dish has origins in the Netherlands and was often called a pannenkoeken or a Bismarck before it made its way to North America in the 1940s.

These puffed-up pancakes are usually served with fresh-squeezed lemon, butter, and powdered sugar, but you know us crowd at ECK—we like to do things just a little different! Our Dutch Baby is covered with the most gorgeous lemon cream glaze, with a few berries added to the top. Perfection!

DUTCH BABY

SERVINGS 4 **SERVING SIZE** ¼ of the Dutch baby and sauce or ¼ of the pancake and sauce

FOR THE PANCAKES

- ½ cup almond flour
- ¼ cup powdered sweetener
- 1 tbsp coconut flour
- pinch salt
- 2 tbsp butter, room temperature
- 4 large eggs
- 1 tsp vanilla
- ¼ cup 35% whipping cream
- 2 tbsp butter, melted, for the pan

FOR THE LEMON CREAM

- 2 oz cream cheese, room temperature
- 2 oz 35% whipping cream
- 2-3 drops food-grade lemon oil
- 3 tbsp powdered sweetener

carbs	fibre	fat	protein
5.75g	2g	38g	11g

1. Preheat oven to 425°F. *note* **Oven must be HOT!**
2. Mix all dry ingredients together, including sweetener.
3. Create a well in the middle of the dry ingredients and add butter. Use a spatula to press the butter into the dry mix; work the dough to ensure the butter is well distributed.
4. Add remaining pancake ingredients and transfer the batter to a blender or food processor; blend until batter is very smooth with no lumps.
5. Rest the batter for at least 10 minutes to give the flour a chance to absorb the liquid and settle.
6. Put a 10-inch cast iron pan into the oven and heat for at least 8 minutes.
7. Remove the skillet from the oven. Handle will be super hot, so use oven mitts!
8. Pour melted butter into the pan and swirl to coat the bottom of the pan.
9. Pour Dutch Baby batter into the hot pan.
10. Bake for 10 minutes at 425°F, then reduce oven to 350°F for the last 5 minutes, for a total of 15 minutes or until pancake has puffed and is golden brown and the sides are beginning to pull away from the skillet.
11. Remove pancake and let cool for about 5 minutes. Drizzle entire pancake with the lemon cream and add berries to the top.
12. Allow to cool slightly. Serve tableside, in the pan.

Eggs Florentine might sound like a lot to put together at first glance, but once you get the hang of this recipe and get used to the process, you'll quickly realize how easy this is to make.

Baked eggs are also known as shirred eggs. Our shirred eggs are baked on a layer of spinach, and topped with a rich hollandaise. Sneak a thin slice of tomato between your spinach and egg for an extra boost of flavour.

EGGS FLORENTINE

SERVINGS 4 **SERVING SIZE** 1 egg and ¼ of the greens

1. Preheat oven to 350°F.
2. Place the oil in a large oven-safe skillet over low heat. Add spinach leaves and cook them for 2 to 3 minutes or until the leaves are wilted. We sometimes add a little water to the pan to help wilt the leaves.
3. Add vinegar, garlic, spices, and the whipping cream if you're using it, and let the mixture simmer for a couple minutes until it starts to thicken slightly.
4. Crack your eggs over the top of the sautéed spinach.
5. Season with salt and pepper and a little Korean chili if you like it spicy, and pop the pan in the oven.
6. Bake until whites are completely set and yolks begin to thicken but are not hard—about 8-10 minutes.

FOR THE SAUCE

1. Add the egg yolks, lemon juice, salt, and cayenne or Tabasco to your stick blender vessel and blend at a medium speed for 20 to 30 seconds.
2. Slowly drizzle the hot butter into the egg yolk mixture, as you continue to blend or pulse at a low speed.
3. Pour the warm Hollandaise over the top of the egg.
4. Serve immediately.

2 tbsp keto-friendly oil

10 cups baby spinach leaves

¼ cup apple cider or white vinegar

2 cloves garlic, minced and salted

½ tsp Korean chili flakes

½ tsp salt

¼ tsp pepper

⅛ tsp nutmeg

¼ cup 35% whipping cream (optional)

4 large eggs

salt and pepper, to season

¼ tsp Korean chili flakes (optional)

4 tomato slices (optional)

FOR THE HOLLANDAISE SAUCE

4 large egg yolks

1 tbsp lemon juice

½ tsp Himalayan pink salt

dash of cayenne pepper or Tabasco sauce

⅔ cup hot melted butter

carbs	fibre	fat	protein
5g	2g	47g	12g

Make sure to cook this enough so that the potato replacement has fully cooked. Adjust cook time according to your own kitchen settings.

We often say that keto is a way of returning to our ancestral way of eating, before there were supermarkets full of packages and preservatives—simply living off the land and consuming the things you grow yourself, such as vegetables, meat, and other animal products from your livestock. Farmer's casserole is a fine example of that; it's a simple breakfast casserole using the ingredients that you would find on a typical farm.

FARMER'S CASSEROLE

SERVINGS 4 **SERVING SIZE** ¼ of the casserole

- 3 cups celeriac or kohlrabi, shredded
- salt and pepper, to season
- ¾ cup shredded Monterey Jack or cheddar cheese
- 1 cup ham, diced
- ¼ cup fresh chives or green onion, minced
- 6 eggs, beaten
- ½ cup 35% whipping cream
- ½ tsp coriander
- ½ tsp Korean chili flakes
- ½ tsp thyme
- ½ tsp salt
- ¼ tsp pepper

1. Grease a baking dish.
2. Arrange potato substitute evenly on bottom of baking dish and season with salt and pepper.
3. Reserving half the cheese for the top, add a layer of cheese, ham, onions.
4. Combine eggs, cream, and seasonings.
5. Pour beaten eggs over top of the casserole.
6. Top with remaining cheese.
7. Refrigerate overnight.
8. Bake at 350°F for 40-50 minutes or until set.
9. Let rest for 5 minutes before serving.

carbs	fibre	fat	protein
8g	4g	30g	15g

Serve with sour cream or your favourite hot sauce.

Chaffles, or cheese waffles have hit the keto community in a fast and furious manner. How could we resist the challenge of creating our very own version of the keto chaffle with our favourite breakfast ingredients?

Our chaffle can be brought back to bare-bones basics without the green onions and ham. How about using these bare-bones chaffles as a holder for all things keto? A sandwich? A burger? You can even add a serving of your favourite keto-friendly sweetener and dress it as a dessert—maybe a sweet version for a strawberry shortcake! The possibilities are endless. What ever route you choose; we're betting you will fall in love with chaffles!

HAM AND GREEN ONION CHAFFLE

SERVINGS 4 **SERVING SIZE** 1 chaffle

- 4 eggs
- 1 cup cheese, grated
- ⅓ cup ham, minced
- ½ cup green onion, diced
- 2 tbsp almond flour
- ½ tsp cream of tartar
- salt and pepper, to taste.

1. Combine all ingredients and place in a waffle maker on medium setting.
2. Cook for about 2 minutes then open the waffle iron to check if the chaffle has reached your desired amount of doneness.

   note **We like our eggs on the lighter side, so 2 minutes is lots for our taste, but your preference might be closer to 3 minutes.**

chaffle fail Be careful not to overload your chaffles with too many ingredients! Our first attempt was so loaded down with ham and green onions that the integrity of the waffle was broken and it fell apart in the waffle maker (see picture.)

to release your chaffle, open the top lid of your waffle maker; gravity will help to remove your cooked chaffle from the grid! Then, instead of trying to scrape off the other side and risk breaking your chaffle apart, turn your waffle maker upside down and release the other side! Works like a charm.

As a variation, remove the onion and ham and instead add sweetener for a dessert-type chaffle! Sliced strawberries and some cream cheese or whipping cream make for a lovely breakfast of strawberry shortcakes.

We topped our chaffle with a dollop of our keto mayonnaise, but you can also use butter or a spoonful of salsa or hot sauce to jazz up your plate.

carbs	fibre	fat	protein
4.25g	0.5g	19g	4.5g

Jiggs Dinner is a traditional Newfoundland dinner of veggies and salted meat, all boiled in the one pot. It would be similar to a New England boiled corned beef dinner. It's often served as an after-church Sunday meal. Every time we make Jiggs Dinner, we make extra so we can have leftovers.

The first feed of leftovers is always hash, but we make sure to save a little of every component of the dish to make some croquettes for a quick and easy breakfast down the road. Fine-tune these croquettes to your own family's liking by switching up the mix of veggies and spice. We like them without much enhancement as we like to taste the Jiggs in every bite.

JIGGS DINNER BREAKFAST CROQUETTES

SERVINGS 16 **SERVING SIZE** 1 croquette

FOR THE CROQUETTE FILLING

- 2 cups cabbage, cooked and diced
- 2 carrots, cooked and diced
- ½ cup salted or corned beef, cooked and diced
- ¼ turnip, cooked and diced
- ½ cup almond flour
- 3 cloves garlic, minced
- 1 medium onion, diced
- 1 tsp parsley, chopped
- 1 tsp thyme
- 1 tsp Korean chili flakes
- 1 tsp salt
- ½ tsp coriander
- ½ tsp cumin
- ½ tsp pepper
- 1 egg, whisked
- 4 oz turkey, chicken, or pork, cooked and minced (optional)

FOR THE EGG WASH

- 1 egg
- ¼ cup water
- salt and pepper

FOR THE CROQUETTE CRUST

- ½ cup almond flour
- ½ cup pork rinds, crushed
- 1 tsp parsley
- 1 tsp thyme
- 1 tsp paprika
- ½ tsp turmeric
- ½ tsp garlic
- ½ tsp pepper
- ½ tsp salt

1. In a large bowl, combine all croquette ingredients. Depending on how you like the consistency of your cakes, you can mash the ingredients slightly or leave them more diced and chunky. Set aside.
2. Measure ¼ cup of mixture then form into a disc or slightly flattened ball. Place on waxed paper. Repeat with remaining mixture.
3. Preheat oven to 450°F. If you're using the convection setting, preheat to 375°F.
4. Prepare a baking sheet with a layer of foil, then a layer of parchment.
5. Whisk the egg wash ingredients together and set aside.
6. Combine ingredients for the crust in a shallow bowl.

Cooked ingredients must not be soggy! If your cooked veggies are wet/damp, place them between sheets of paper towel or a clean kitchen towel and wring them out.

Croquettes can be sprayed generously with olive oil, to increase the crunch factor. We use a refillable oil sprayer and spray them at the 10-minute mark.

carbs	fibre	fat	protein
4g	1.5g	6.6g	5.5g

7. Arrange your components in the following order on your work space for ease of assembly:
    1. uncoated croquettes
    2. egg wash
    3. crumb/crust mixture
    4. baking sheet
8. Dip each croquette in the egg mixture, then into the crumb mixture, pressing the coating into the disc, and then place on the prepared cooking sheet.
9. Bake in the oven about 15 minutes, or until golden.

Serve with leftover turkey gravy or keto-friendly ketchup. You can find our recipe for ketchup in our first book on page 228.

Remember the patty-style hash browns you got in that take-out breakfast? This is our replacement for those. Have them plain with just the potato replacement, or have them dressed to the nines with alternate spices and dipping sauces, depending on your family's preferences.

KETO HASH BROWNS

SERVINGS 8 **SERVING SIZE** 1 hash brown

¼ cup keto-friendly oil
3 cups celeriac, shredded or diced
3 tbsp onion, minced
2 eggs
1 tbsp parsley
1 tbsp coconut flour
1 tsp garlic powder
1 tsp salt
dash hot sauce (optional)

1. Mix all ingredients (except oil) and form into patties.
2. Add oil to a large sauté pan over medium heat.
3. Carefully drop patties into the hot oil.
4. Fry for about 3-4 minutes or until golden brown, then flip to brown the other side.
5. Turn heat down and continue to cook for another 4-5 minutes to finish cooking the other side of your hash brown.

note Cook time will vary depending on how thick you make your patties.

If you like it spicy, try this alternate spice mix:

1 tbsp paprika
2 tsp oregano
2 tsp thyme
2 tsp garlic powder
2 tsp onion powder
1 tsp chipotle spice
1 tsp coriander

We use two spatulas to tidy the edges of our hash brown after dropping them into the pan.

carbs	fibre	fat	protein
4.75g	0.75g	9.5g	3g

Toutons were a staple for most Newfoundland families. Like most breads, they were a cheap way to stretch the budget and provide something to fill up hungry bellies.

Toutons are often made from leftover bread dough, or dough that was left to rise overnight. These pancakes were most often fried on the stovetop, but they could also be deep fried or cooked over a fire/grill like bannock. They are known by many names across the province: tiffins, damper dogs, bang belly or flats, among others.

They were traditionally served with molasses, but that wouldn't be keto, as molasses is burnt sugar! Instead, we recommend you use our toutons for sopping up egg yolks, or even cut in half for a breakfast sandwich.

NEWFOUNDLAND TOUTONS

SERVINGS 6 **SERVING SIZE** 1 touton

- ⅔ cup almond flour
- 1 tsp powdered sweetener
- ½ tsp cream of tartar
- ¼ tsp baking soda
- ¼ tsp Xanthan gum
- ¼ tsp salt
- ¾ cup (150 g) mozzarella cheese, melted
- 1 large egg
- oil, for frying

1. Mix all dry ingredients.
2. Add the still-warm melted cheese and the egg, and mix with your hands until the dough is fully combined.
3. Set dough in the fridge for at least 15 minutes to allow time for the ingredients to come together.
4. Remove dough from the fridge. Roll the dough into 2- to 3-oz balls and then flatten them into discs.
5. Add oil to a medium-size pan over medium-high heat.
6. When the oil is hot, place the dough discs in the pan and cover. Reduce heat to low. We want to slow down the browning on the outside to allow the middle of our dough to cook through.
7. After 3-5 minutes your dough should be starting to get golden brown on the bottom.
8. Flip the discs to cook the other side. Cover.
9. Cook for about 5 more minutes or until your toutons are cooked through and golden on each side.

carbs	fibre	fat	protein
3.7g	2g	15g	8.5g

Serve alongside a runny egg, with our keto maple syrup (see recipe on page 208 in our first book) or with a dollop of your favourite berry compote.

CUP OF
SUNSHINE

Geoff and I were together almost 10 years when he finally asked for peanut butter cookies! My immediate response was, "What?!? You like peanut butter?!? How could I not know this after all this time?"

As funny as it sounds, this one was a dilemma for me as I'm not a fan of PB, and...well, Geoff and I pretty much share everything in life—we like it that way. I did enjoy an old fashioned PB&J sandwich back in the day; I think the jelly part helped to tame that full-peanut flavour for me. So, my mind started to do the thing that it does: spinning and troubleshooting... creating.

A sandwich didn't cut it for me—too pedestrian. My mind spun with ideas to jazz this one up and make it a glorious keto thing. I started to think of how my grandfather used warm jam on his pancakes and the proverbial lightbulb suddenly went on, shining brightly. PB&J pancakes to the rescue!

Don't make these fellas too big or they will be difficult to flip. Now you can have your kid-approved fave and share it with your family for breakfast.

PEANUT BUTTER 'N' JELLY PANCAKES

SERVINGS 10 **SERVING SIZE** 1 pancake

FOR THE JAM

- 1 cup berries—we use a combination of raspberries and blackcurrants, but you can use any berry
- ½ cup water
- ⅛ cup apple cider vinegar
- ¼ cup powdered sweetener, to taste
- ⅛ tsp salt

FOR THE PANCAKES

- 1 cup almond flour
- ¼ cup powdered sweetener, to taste
- ½ tsp baking soda
- ¼ tsp salt
- ½ cup 35% whipping cream
- 2 eggs
- ¼ cup natural peanut butter—we use smooth PB but you can use crunchy if that's your preference
- 1 tsp vanilla extract
- oil, for frying

1. Add all jam ingredients to a saucepan over medium-low heat and simmer/reduce 'til the berries have stewed and reached your desired consistency. It should resemble a thick warm jam. Add extra water if needed.
2. In a medium-size mixing bowl, combine all dry ingredients for the pancake. We whisk them through and then use the bottom of a measuring cup to flatten/squish any lumps of flour.
3. Add wet ingredients to the batter and whisk to fully combine. We also used a spatula here, squishing and pressing into the batter to ensure no big pieces of stubborn PB resisted being stirred in.
4. Turn on your burner to medium-high heat. When the pan has heated up, add your oil, and allow it to get hot.

   note **Re-oil your pan as needed; don't let your pan dry out.**

carbs	fibre	fat	protein
7g	3g	18g	6.6g

Double or triple your recipe and save these for a 'take-out' breakfast. Take out of the fridge/freezer already made!

5. Spoon your batter into the pan and then turn your heat back to medium-low. The initial heat allows your pancake to seal over; turning down the heat ensures they don't burn while cooking through.

   note **Don't make these too big; we use a ¼ cup measure to dole out batter.**

6. Cook for 2-3 minutes and then flip and repeat.

   note **Pancakes usually bubble when they're cooked and ready to flip! Look for the telltale bubbles; they will tell you when to do that initial flip.**

7. Plate your PB pancakes and pour the jam over the top! Enjoy!

As a variation, use these cooled PB pancakes as bread; add a layer of jelly between pancakes/slices and create PB&J sandwiches—a perfect lunch or snack.

Let's Dive In

In Newfoundland cooking, soups and stews were a staple. They were cheap and easy and often full of potatoes and other fillers. If company came to visit, you added water to stretch the broth so more mouths could be fed with the same amount of food.

Then there is the age-old question: are potatoes supposed to go into a soup, or only in stew? Do you add them if your intention is to freeze the soup? So much fuss about what is supposed to be a simple broth with spices, veggies, and meat.

The rules for soups and stews are much less complicated when you take potatoes out of the equation for keto living. We have faux-tato replacements, and they're more than welcome in any pot of ours.

SOUPS & BROTHS

Broccoli and Cheese Soup | 82

Clam Chowder | 85

French Onion Soup | 86

Kohlrabi and Green Onion Soup | 89

Lobster Bisque | 90

Nanny Wazzer's Chicken Soup | 92

Roasted Red Pepper Soup | 95

Tomato Parmesan Soup with Grilled Cheese | 96

All macro counts given are per serving.

Back in my pre-keto days, broccoli and cheddar soup was one of my indulgences, especially on a cool crisp fall day. It was one of those guilty pleasures that I would quickly devour, savouring every drop. Then I would immediately feel guilty and bad about myself for the rest of the day. That's no fun!

That ooey, gooey, cheesy broth, loaded up with the earthy taste of broccoli and just enough bacon to satisfy the need for crunch—how could a girl resist? It often made me wonder why everything that tastes good was so bad for you! Then I found keto, and that problem disappeared.

This guilt-free keto version is thickened with just a touch of Xanthan gum and cream cheese, but you can omit the Xanthan and just reduce. You will be pleasantly surprised at how downright decadent and delicious this soup tastes either way.

BROCCOLI AND CHEESE SOUP

SERVINGS 4 **SERVING SIZE** 1 bowl

- ⅛ cup white onion, diced
- 2 tbsp butter
- ½ tsp garlic, finely minced
- 2 cups chicken broth
- 1 cup broccoli, diced
- ¼ cup 35% whipping cream
- 1 tbsp cream cheese
- 1 cup cheddar cheese, shredded
- salt and pepper, to taste
- ½ tsp Xanthan gum, for thickening (optional)
- 2 slices cooked bacon, crumbled, for garnish

1. In a large pot, sauté onion with butter over medium heat, until translucent.
2. Add garlic and cook for 2 minutes more, being careful not to burn the garlic.
3. Add broth and broccoli to pot and cook until broccoli is tender. Reduce heat to simmer.
4. Stir whipping cream and cream cheese into soup, and continue to simmer until cream cheese has dissolved completely.
5. Turn off heat and stir in cheddar cheese.
6. Add salt and pepper to taste.
7. Sprinkle in Xanthan gum, if using, and wait for the soup to thicken. Easy does it!
8. Serve hot with bacon crumbles and grated cheese.

carbs	fibre	fat	protein
3g	1g	24g	12g

We usually cook this in a huge double or triple batch and freeze the extras for a quick meal or two later in the year. This recipe is excellent keto for any day of the year.

FAMILY GARDEN
since 1972
HERBS & SPICES
fresh & natural

This is a super-easy East Coast favourite. Any seafood can be substituted for the clams here, but we think the clams add a special flair to this chowder—especially when you add the shells for that fancy presentation.

Clam chowder can be made a day or so ahead of time and stored in the fridge for a quick warm-up.

CLAM CHOWDER

SERVINGS 4 **SERVING SIZE** 1 bowl

- 2 tbsp bacon fat or equivalent oil
- 1 medium onion, diced
- 4 pieces of bacon or salt beef, chopped into ½-inch pieces
- 3 cloves of garlic, minced
- 1 carrot, grated
- 1 tsp thyme
- ½ tsp parsley
- ½ tsp oregano
- ½ tsp Newfoundland (summer) savoury, or thyme
- 2 pinches nutmeg
- salt and pepper, to taste
- 1 cup white wine, or ¾ cup extra broth and ¼ cup apple cider vinegar
- 2 tbsp fish sauce
- 12 oz clams—we use a combination of shelled and in the shell
- 3 cups chicken or fish broth
- 2 cups clam juice
- ½ cup 35% whipping cream
- 1 tsp Xanthan gum
- cooked bacon and chopped green onion for garnish

1. Preheat a large stockpot over medium heat.
2. Add onions and sauté in fat until translucent.
3. Add salt beef, garlic, and carrot, and sauté for another 3-5 minutes.
4. Push garlic and onions back to the edges of the pan and add spices directly into the oil in the centre of the pan. This will allow the spices to bloom.
5. Add wine and fish sauce.
6. Add clams, broth, and clam juice, and simmer for 15 minutes.
7. Add whipping cream and slowly sprinkle in Xanthan gum. Simmer for 5-10 minutes.
8. Garnish with cooked bacon and green onion. Serve hot.

We keep our Xanthan gum in a shaker and sprinkle it into a pot a little bit at a time. Xanthan gum thickens as it cools, so use a gentle hand with this ingredient.

carbs	fibre	fat	protein
9g	1g	23g	18g

French onion soup is the perfect dish to serve your friends on a cold winter night. A traditional French onion soup would use more onions that we do in this keto version; we reduced ours by half to cut down on the amount of carbs. You get all the flavour, without blowing your macros.

Two-Minute Bread (page 250 in our first book) can be made ahead of time and placed on top of the soup in the individual ramekins before topping with cheese, but we prefer just the broth.

FRENCH ONION SOUP

SERVINGS 4   **SERVING SIZE** 1 bowl

4 tbsp butter

2 medium onions, thinly sliced

8 cups beef broth

½ sherry or white wine

2 tbsp fish sauce

1 tsp thyme

½ tsp parsley

Himalayan pink salt and black pepper to taste

1 oz grated *gruyère* cheese, per bowl

1. Add butter to a large stockpot.
2. Add and sauté onions while stirring, until the onions are a medium brown colour.

   note **Remember, brown means flavour, so don't be afraid to let the onions really brown up. Be careful not to let them burn, though!**
3. Add broth, wine/sherry, fish sauce and spices, and allow the soup to come to a boil.
4. Add salt and pepper to taste.
5. Reduce heat and simmer for 10 minutes.
6. Spoon soup into individual ramekins and sprinkle cheese over the top.
7. Place the ramekins on a cookie sheet and then under the broiler for 3-5 minutes or until cheese is bubbly.

carbs	fibre	fat	protein
6g	1g	28g	10g

Xanthan gum can be sprinkled in to slightly thicken the soup.

Cloud bread or any other keto-friendly bread can be used to top the soup.

In our pre-keto days, kohlrabi was just a funky-looking vegetable that we ignored every week at the grocery store. We didn't know what it tasted like, nor did we even care. We discovered this multi-purpose veggie during our search for the perfect keto-friendly fry; while it stood up to the French-fry test, it was in this soup that it really revealed its full flavour to us.

KOHLRABI AND GREEN ONION SOUP

SERVINGS 4 **SERVING SIZE** 1 bowl

2 tbsp olive oil

⅛ tsp Korean chili flakes, crushed

1 cup chopped green onion, white and light green parts only—keep dark green part for garnish or for use in future soup stock

4 cloves of garlic, minced

salt and pepper, to taste

2 cups kohlrabi, greens and stems removed, cut into ½-inch-thick chunks

4 cups vegetable or chicken broth

½ tsp ginger, grated

pinch of nutmeg

½ tsp dried thyme

½ tsp dried parsley

1 cup 35% whipping cream

FOR GARNISH

olive oil

green onion tops, minced

1. Heat the olive oil in a large pot over medium heat. Add the Korean chili flakes, green onion, and garlic. Cook until the onions are translucent, about 5 minutes.
2. Add the salt and pepper, kohlrabi, and broth. Bring to a boil. Reduce heat and simmer for 25 minutes.
3. Grate in the ginger and add herbs in the last 5 minutes of cooking.
4. Let cool slightly and purée the soup with a stick blender until smooth. Add extra seasonings as needed.
5. Add cream and reheat the soup, but don't bring to a boil.

We always have a batch of this in our freezer for quick and easy lunches. We omit the cream for the freezer batches and instead add it when we're reheating and getting ready to serve.

carbs	fibre	fat	protein
7.5g	3g	30g	2.5g

We lined our sieve with a couple of layers of cheesecloth to ensure no pieces of shell made it into the final dish.

In my earlier years I often made this bisque, but made the mistake of throwing out the lobster shells. It was years later that I discovered that I was throwing out the part that had the most flavour! You can make this bisque with just the shells, or you can do a lobster soup without roasting and using the shells. However, it's in combining the two that you get the full depth of flavour here.

A *bisque* is a smooth, creamy, highly seasoned soup of French origin, classically based on a strained broth of crustacean, so you can use crab, lobster, crawfish, shrimp, or prawns.

LOBSTER BISQUE

SERVINGS 4 **SERVING SIZE** 1 bowl

- 1 or 2 lobster shells
- olive oil, to coat the shells
- 1 tbsp butter
- 1 carrot, chopped
- 1 medium onion, chopped
- 1 stalk of celery, chopped
- 2 tbsp tomato paste
- 3 cloves garlic, minced
- 2 cups of fish, chicken, or veggie broth
- 1 tsp dried thyme
- Himalayan pink salt, and pepper, to taste
- 1 tsp smoked paprika
- 1 cup dry white wine.
- 1 cup 35% whipping cream
- 1 tsp Xanthan gum

FOR GARNISH

- ¼ cup of cooked lobster, per serving
- chives or green onion, chopped

carbs	fibre	fat	protein
9.25g	1.75g	31g	17g

1. Crush the lobster shells and coat in olive oil.

   note **We crush our shells by putting them between layers of a clean tea towel and hitting them with a hammer or rolling pin.**

2. Bake in a 350°F oven for 10 to 30 minutes, taking care not to scorch the shells. This step will deepen the flavour of the broth tremendously. Set aside.
3. Add butter, carrot, and onion to a large stockpot and sauté the veggies until they are tender.
4. Add celery and tomato paste and continue to cook for 15 minutes.
5. Add garlic and broth to the pot and continue to simmer until all ingredients are cooked and tender.
6. Let the mixture cool slightly, then blend with an immersion blender or bullet.
7. Add the crushed shells, seasonings (except garnish) and wine to the stockpot and cover. Simmer for 1 hour, or until the rich briny taste of the lobster is infused throughout the broth.
8. Remove from heat and pour all ingredients through a fine sieve to remove any pieces of shell or bits of veggies.
9. Return to the pot and stir in whipping cream; add Xanthan gum to thicken.

   note **We keep our Xanthan gum in a shaker and sprinkle it into a pot a little bit at a time. Xanthan gum thickens as it cools, so use a gentle hand with this ingredient.**

10. Dress each individual bowl with pieces of lobster and top with chives or green onion.

There is nothing in this world as comforting as Nan's chicken soup. Added to that for me are memories of sitting in Nan's kitchen with her fussing over everybody, refilling bowls, and taking it all in, as the whole family demolished bowl after bowl of soup.

Her name wasn't Nanny Wazzer, it was Dwyer, but one of the grandkids, my niece Jillian, couldn't get her mouth around the surname, and Wazzer was all she could manage. After that, it just became Nanny Wazzer for us all.

I like my vegetables cut in a rustic manner, but Geoff likes his veggies cut smaller. I play and tease him that he's old and needs geriatric soup, all chopped up tiny...but it's really all about what you're used to.

This one had double the pleasure for our family; hubby Geoff was the boy next door, so he too had been lucky enough to taste and enjoy my grandmother's soup way back when. The look on his face and what he said when he tried this keto version? "You nailed it!!"

Priceless.

NANNY WAZZER'S CHICKEN SOUP

SERVINGS 12 **SERVING SIZE** 1 bowl

- 2 tbsp oil
- 8 chicken thighs, with bones and skin
- 1 medium onion, diced
- 1 tbsp thyme
- 1 tsp Newfoundland (summer) savoury
- ½ cup water, to deglaze
- 1 lb salt meat, cut into 1-inch cubes
- 4 cups chicken broth
- 6 cups of water
- 1 tsp turmeric
- 1 tsp salt
- 1 tsp pepper
- 3 cloves garlic, minced
- ½ daikon radish, cubed
- 2 medium carrots, diced
- ½ medium turnip, diced
- ½ cup apple cider vinegar
- 1 can (28 oz) San Marzano tomatoes—any clean canned tomatoes can be used
- 1 package of shirataki rice or konjac pasta, cut into bite-sized pieces for noodles

1. Place oil in a preheated large stockpot over medium-high heat.
2. Add chicken and cook, turning it often to brown each side, to bring out the full flavour.

   note **You don't want the meat to burn, but allow it to get good and crispy on the edges. It will probably stick to the bottom of the pan, but we will deglaze that later in the cooking.**

3. Add onion and use a spoon or spatula to move it right onto the bottom of the pan among the chicken pieces.
4. Add thyme and savoury.
5. When the bottom of the pot is good and brown and the chicken is mostly cooked through, add the water to deglaze the pot. Use a metal spoon to scrape off all the tasty brown bits.

carbs	fibre	fat	protein
7.3g	2.3g	19g	19g

As your soup is cooking, top up with extra water as you see fit. We all have different tastes, and some will like a thicker soup while others will prefer more broth.

6. Add the salt meat when the water has reduced; allow the salt meat to sauté on the bottom of the pan with the chicken and onion. We allow the salt beef to take most of the bottom of the pan here, and push the chicken back to the edges of the pan.
7. Continue to cook for about 10 minutes.
8. Add chicken broth, water, turmeric, salt, pepper, and garlic.
9. Bring soup to a boil and then reduce to medium heat to simmer.
10. Add daikon radish and cook for 10 minutes.
11. Add carrot and turnip and let the soup continue to simmer until all veggies are cooked through.
12. Add apple cider vinegar and tomatoes; cook for at least 30 minutes, to allow the vinegar to mellow.
13. Remove chicken pieces from the broth, cut chicken into bite-size pieces, and remove any bones.
14. Return chicken to the pot and add konjac noodles or shirataki rice.
15. Simmer for another 5 minutes and serve.

note **Leaving the bones in until it's ready to serve will add to the collagen in the broth.**

This is an absolutely delicious keto take on a decadent and spicy soup. We've always loved red pepper soup but quickly realized that everything commercially available is full of uglies. The only way around this situation was to knit our own recipe.

Roasting the peppers helps to draw out extra flavours from the vegetables, but it's not absolutely necessary to the recipe. You will get lots of flavour from the peppers on their own; the extra step of roasting just adds an extra boost to the depth of flavour.

This soup is perfect for a cold winters' day. Make sure to give this a good blend with an immersion blender to fully incorporate all the flavours and oils.

ROASTED RED PEPPER SOUP

SERVINGS 4 **SERVING SIZE** 1 bowl

- 4 red peppers, scorched, cooled, and seeds removed
- 2 tbsp butter
- 2 tbsp olive oil
- 1 medium onion, chopped
- 3 cloves garlic, minced
- 2 tsp oregano, minced
- 1 tsp thyme
- 1 tsp smoked paprika
- 1 tsp ginger
- 1 tsp Korean chili flakes
- 1 tsp Himalayan pink salt
- ½ tsp black pepper
- ½ cup white wine
- 1 tbsp apple cider vinegar
- ¼ cup tomato paste
- 6 cups broth

FOR GARNISH

- ¼ cup 35 % whipping cream
- Parmesan cheese, grated
- fresh parsley leaves

1. Roast bell peppers until blackened all over, by placing them over a gas burner. You can also use a grill or oven broiler.
2. Transfer the peppers to a covered bowl and steam for 5 minutes.
3. Remove the skins, ribs, and seeds. Chop the peppers roughly.
4. In a Dutch oven or large stockpot over medium heat, heat the butter and olive oil. Add the onions and cook until translucent, about 5 minutes.
5. Add garlic and spices, and cook for 3 more minutes.
6. Add peppers and turn up heat to brown them on the bottom of the pan.
7. Use the white wine and vinegar to deglaze the pan.
8. Stir the tomato paste right into the bottom of the pot and cook for 2 more minutes.
9. Add broth.
10. Bring the mixture to a gentle boil, then reduce the heat to medium-low.
11. Let cool slightly then blend using an immersion blender or purée it in a regular blender.
12. Taste and adjust seasonings. Serve with a swirl of cream, grated Parmesan, and fresh parsley.

Extra broth may be added to make the soup a little thinner, if that is your preference.

carbs	fibre	fat	protein
12.5g	3.5g	20g	3g

It's a cold day and you're 10 years old; you just came back from skating, you're frozen to the core, and you're starving. Mom to the rescue! She whips up some tomato soup (chances are it's from a tin) and a grilled cheese sandwich that's gooey and cheesy inside and crispy-crunchy on the outside. Heaven and pure comfort in every bite, am I right?!

I don't know why this particular combination of food hits the spot as much it does, but I know in my keto life, there was many a cold day I would have loved a warm-up over a bowl with a sandwich alongside. Especially if it could be served by my own Momma.

Make the bread ahead of time so it's ready to be assembled while you're letting your soup rest. Hoping this recipe will help to make memories for you and your family!

TOMATO PARMESAN SOUP *with* GRILLED CHEESE

SANDWICH SERVINGS 1 **SOUP SERVINGS** 6

FOR THE BREAD

3 tbsp almond flour
½ tsp cream of tartar
¼ tsp Xanthan gum
¼ tsp baking soda
pinch salt
1 tbsp butter, melted
1 egg

FOR THE SOUP

1 tbsp keto-friendly oil
½ onion, diced
4 cloves garlic, minced
1 tsp oregano
1 tsp thyme
½ tsp parsley
½ tsp basil
½ tsp rosemary
½ tsp Korean chili flakes
4 cups chicken broth
1 can (28 oz) San Marzano tomatoes
1 cup tomato sauce
2 Parmesan heels (optional)
2 cups spinach, packed
½ cup Parmesan, freshly grated
Himalayan pink salt, and pepper, to taste

FOR THE GRILLED CHEESE

2 slices of microwave bread (see above)
2 tsp mayo (see recipe on page 227 in our first book) or butter
1 tsp Dijon mustard
1 slice (or 1 oz) real Swiss cheese
1 slice (or 1 oz) real cheddar cheese

FOR THE BREAD

1. Combine all dry ingredients. Cream in the butter and then stir in the egg.
2. Microwave for 90 seconds. Let cool and slice in half.

FOR THE SOUP

1. In a large stockpot over medium high heat, add the oil and onions and cook for about 3 minutes or until they begin to turn translucent.
2. Add garlic and spices and cook for another minute, keeping an eye to make sure the garlic doesn't burn.
3. Add broth, tomatoes, tomato sauce and Parmesan heels and bring to a boil, then turn back the heat to a low simmer. Continue to simmer for about 10 minutes.
4. Add the spinach. Cook until the spinach has wilted and is completely cooked through.
5. Add the Parmesan cheese and remove from heat. Cover and let stand for 5 minutes.
6. Pulse soup with a stick blender until it reaches your preferred consistency. We like ours with the tomatoes mostly puréed, with a slightly textured consistency.

7. Adjust salt and pepper to taste.

FOR THE GRILLED CHEESE

1. Spread a thin layer of mayo on the outside of both bread slices and lay one piece of bread, mayo/butter side down, in the preheated sauté pan. You can use butter, but the mayo will give you the best flavour and browning.
2. While it's in the pan, use a small spatula to spread Dijon on the top of this piece of bread, then top with cheeses; finally, top it with the other piece of bread, butter side up.
3. Turn your burner back to low-medium and place a cover on the pan.

   note **A clear glass cover is ideal here, as you can watch the cheese melt without uncovering it and losing the trapped heat. The idea is to help melt the cheese inside the sandwich with the trapped heat, which will help it stick together. Keep an eye on it to make sure your bread is not burning.**

4. After about 3 minutes, or when the cheese has melted and the bread is golden brown, use two egg turners to lift your sandwich.
5. Place one on the bottom underneath the sandwich, another on the top of your sandwich upside-down, and wedge/trap the sandwich between the two flippers.
6. Gripping firmly and acting fast, flip the sandwich right-side up. Place the uncooked side of the sandwich back down into the pan and cook 'til it's golden brown.
7. Remove to a cutting board. Let cool slightly and then slice and plate alongside a bowl of soup.

SOUP

carbs	fibre	fat	protein
10.8g	2.3g	6g	7g

SANDWICH

carbs	fibre	fat	protein
6g	2g	52g	26g

Look to the Sea

In Newfoundland, when one is referring to fish it usually means cod; any other references will name the specific fish, such as salmon, tuna, or trout. If you go into a local restaurant and see fish on the menu, chances are it's going to be codfish. This is a reflection of the importance of cod to Newfoundland history and culture; it's an understood thing, if you're from here.

Our island home was originally settled because of the abundance of codfish in our waters. History has it that that when European explorer Giovanni Caboto—known as John Cabot in English—and his crew first arrived on the coast of what is now called Newfoundland, fish was so plentiful that they could lower a basket into the ocean and raise it to find the basket teeming with fish. In 1497 Cabot returned home as a hero. Not only had he encountered a land largely unknown to Europeans, but he had also found a seemingly endless supply of codfish.

SEAFOOD

Butter-Poached Cod | 100

Crab Cakes | 103

Curried Cod | 104

ECK Prosciutto-Wrapped Sole | 107

Grilled Calamari | 108

Lobster Risotto | 111

Lobster Roll | 112

Pan-Seared Scallops with Celeriac | 115

Salmon with Dijon Glaze | 116

Tomato-Butter Glazed Salmon | 119

All macro counts given are per serving.

Geoff was gone out to a fancy restaurant: a must-attend work function with some bigwig execs. He confessed he would rather stay home, but was looking forward to a free meal...it wasn't all bad. I was left to my own devices, so this delightful dish happened. The kicker of it was, the bigwigs were all drooling over the picture of my supper (that I had sent Geoff) instead of what was on their own plates!

If you're a lover of white fish, this is one you just gotta try! The butter that is used for poaching adds to the flavour of the cod, and also adds a level of smooth velvety luxury to the fish.

Make this recipe your own. Swap out the spices, add baby tomatoes or other tender veggies. You really can't go wrong!

BUTTER-POACHED COD

SERVINGS 4 **SERVING SIZE** ¼ pound of cod

- 1 cup butter, melted
- ¼ cup white wine
- 1 clove garlic, smashed
- 3 sprigs thyme
- 1 lb cod fillets, cut into uniform pieces
- salt and pepper, to season

Oil can be used to top-up.

carbs	fibre	fat	protein
0.8g	0g	12g	14g

OVEN METHOD

1. Preheat oven to 325°F.
2. Season fish with salt and pepper.
3. Add butter, white wine, garlic to oven-safe baking dish.
4. Add fish and herb garnish. Top up the butter so that the fish is completely covered. Place the dish in oven uncovered.
5. Cook fish until opaque, 10-15 minutes.

STOVETOP METHOD

1. Heat butter, white wine, garlic, and thyme in a large saucepan over medium-low heat.

   Note Do not let the liquid boil. It should stay between 160°F and 180°F and you should see very few bubbles. Keep an eye to make sure it stays at a simmer. Adjust temperature here if needed.

2. When the liquid is nearly simmering, add seasoned fish fillets. The liquid should fully cover the fish.
3. Cook fish until opaque, 10-15 minutes.

Pour some of the poaching liquid over the fish when you're plating, for extra decadence.

Serve with roasted, steamed or sautéed veggies.

This is a classic East Coast crab cake with a keto twist. It's similar to one you would have mixed with potato pre-keto.

note **If you prefer a cake with a higher crab content, cut the almond flour in half or increase the crab meat by ½ cup.**

The meatier these are, the more delicate the cakes are, so take care when flipping and moving them around in the pan.

CRAB CAKES

SERVINGS 6 **SERVING SIZE** 1 crab cake

1. Preheat oven to 275°F.
2. Boil the cauliflower and then use paper towels to remove the excess water. *note* **This is a crucial step. If there is a lot of water left in the cauliflower, the crab cakes won't hold together.**
3. Blend cauliflower in a bullet or blender. Set aside.
4. Reserving the crab, combine all other ingredients thoroughly.
5. Gently fold in the crab with a spatula or spoon and then assemble crab cakes. Cook over medium heat in an oiled sauté pan for 3-5 minutes on each side or until golden brown.
6. Transfer to the oven to finish and cook for 10 minutes.

- 1 cup cauliflower rice, finely riced
- 2 large eggs
- ½ cup almond flour
- 2 tbsp mayo
- 1 tbsp parsley
- 1½ tsp salt
- 1 tsp Dijon mustard
- 1 tsp fish sauce
- 1 tsp paprika
- 1 tsp garlic powder
- 1 tsp tarragon
- pinch nutmeg
- 12-16 oz crab meat, precooked and diced
- olive oil, for frying

Don't overfill the pan, and re-grease as needed.

Make certain to squeeze all the water out of the cauliflower for a good consistency. We use a paper towel and also place it in a clean kitchen towel and wring it out.

Serve with Hollandaise, tartar sauce, or butter. Any faux-tato replacement can be used instead of cauliflower.

carbs	fibre	fat	protein
4g	2.25g	20g	21g

Curry take-aways are huge in the UK. Coming from a culture where take-outs are primarily fish and chips, it was one of the things that surprised me on my first visit across the pond. Instead of ordering out for a pizza or Chinese food, it's all about the curries.

Curried cod surprised me, too! I was expecting to hate it, but I gotta admit, I was no match for the delicate cod surrounded by coconut milk and rich curry spices.

Give this recipe a try! It's delicious as either a main with a purée or keto-friendly rice on the side, or as a small-plate appetizer to set the tone for a delicious meal.

CURRIED COD

SERVINGS 4 **SERVING SIZE** 4 oz cod

- 1 lb cod
- ¼ cup lemon juice
- 2 cloves garlic, minced
- ½ cup coconut milk
- ¼ cup olive oil
- 1½ tbsp curry powder
- ½ tsp turmeric
- pinch nutmeg
- ¼ tsp Korean chili flakes
- salt and pepper, to taste
- 1 bell pepper, diced
- 1 carrot, julienned
- 4 green onions, chopped
- ¼ cup fresh basil or parsley, chopped for garnish

1. Preheat oven to 400°F.
2. Prepare cod by drying off the individual pieces and then drizzling the lemon juice over the top. Set aside.
3. Combine garlic, coconut milk, oil, curry powder, turmeric, nutmeg, Korean chili flakes, and salt and pepper in a medium-size baking dish.
4. Add the bell pepper, carrot, and green onions. Stir until vegetables are fully coated.
5. Cover the baking dish and cook for 15 minutes.
6. Remove the pan from the oven and add fish to the curry sauce; replace lid and return to the oven.
7. Bake for 15 minutes longer, or until fish flakes easily and is cooked through.
8. Serve alongside cauliflower rice or daikon/celeriac mash.

carbs	fibre	fat	protein
7.25g	3g	16g	21g

We are huge fans of cooking shows and are often inspired by the food created by contestants. In one episode of a show we enjoy, one of the competing chefs cooked a John Dory sole that was wrapped in prosciutto and sage. We were very intrigued with the combination. It was so far removed from the typical fish and chips that we were used to, and it looked downright delicious!

The wrapped fish was the winning dish for the food challenge in the episode, with the winning chef rewarded by having their dish (and themselves) featured in a fancy culinary magazine. Of course, when we tried to find the recipe to make it for ourselves, it was nowhere to be found. So, we knit our own.

After many attempts and different combinations of herbs we settled on this simple rendition. We hope your family likes it as much as we do.

ECK PROSCIUTTO-WRAPPED SOLE

SERVINGS 4 **SERVING SIZE** 4 oz whitefish

Two 8 oz portions of sole, cod, or other whitefish, at room temperature

½ tsp pepper

½ tsp garlic powder

½ tsp tarragon

12-16 slices of prosciutto

2 tbsp oil, for frying

1. Pat fillets dry and sprinkle with a little pepper, garlic powder, and tarragon. You don't need any salt here as the prosciutto is already salty.
2. Carefully wrap the fish in prosciutto. If you're using sheets it should be super easy, but if you're using strips you will have to overlap them to create a full single sheet.
3. Add oil to your medium-size oven-proof skillet; have burner on medium heat.
4. When the oil is hot, add the wrapped fish seam-side down and cook for about 2 minutes per side to seal the outside.
5. Transfer the pan to the oven and continue to cook for 10-15 minutes until the fish is completely cooked through and is at an internal temperature of 140 to 160°F.

Try this as fish sticks! Cut the fish into one-inch strips and wrap them in prosciutto. Serve this with our Miss Bobbi's Chips (recipe on page 38). Delicious!

carbs	fibre	fat	protein
0.25g	0g	23g	52g

Calamari is one of those foods that do well with either a quick flash in the pan, or a long and slow cook, both of which will give you a tender, succulent meat. The in-between is where you will find those rubbery little rings that were probably served to you years ago.

This is a quick and easy-peasy dish. It's a great starter for a family BBQ or as finger food for when friends gather; or, serve it as a main, with grilled or roasted veggies. Delish!

GRILLED CALAMARI

SERVINGS 8 **SERVING SIZE** 4 oz

- 1½ lbs calamari rings
- 2 tbsp oil
- 1 tsp Himalayan pink or sea salt
- 1 tsp pepper
- 1 tsp Korean chili flakes
- 1 tsp parsley, tarragon, thyme, or oregano
- 3 cloves garlic, minced
- lemon juice to finish

1. Dry calamari with paper towel.
2. Combine all ingredients in a bowl and mix well to fully coat the calamari.
3. Grill for 3 minutes over high heat, turning at the mid-way mark.
4. To finish, transfer from the grill to a bowl, splash the lemon juice over the calamari, and check seasoning.
5. Serve immediately.

carbs	fibre	fat	protein
4.3g	0.5g	6.3g	18g

We grilled ours right in the cast iron pan!

Our little risotto recipe is inspired by British television star Gordon Ramsay, and also a tribute to my own dear old Dad.

Dad often benefits from the abundance of cooked keto items produced as we're testing recipes here in the ECK kitchen. We often send him home loaded down with frozen containers and freezer bags of food. He rarely complains. When we were ready to kitchen-test this recipe, we made sure he was right there with us, as we know just how much he loves lobster. We wanted to make sure he tried it fresh, in all its glory.

This one got two thumbs up and was awarded the 'Dad-approved badge.' He swears he will happily sacrifice himself for this dish anytime.

LOBSTER RISOTTO

SERVINGS 6 **SERVING SIZE** ½ cup

- 1 package konjac rice
- 2 tbsp olive oil
- 1 medium onion, diced
- 3 cloves garlic, minced
- ½ cup dry white wine
- ⅔ cup lobster stock, chicken, or veggie broth
- ¼ cup 35% whipping cream
- ¼ cup tomato sauce
- ½ cup tomatoes, diced
- ⅛ tsp sea salt, to taste
- 1 pinch pepper, to taste
- 1 tsp fresh parsley, chopped
- 1 lb lobster, precooked, cut into pieces—reserve tail for plating/garnish

TO FINISH

- 4 tbsp butter
- 3 tbsp chives, finely chopped
- ½ cup Parmesan cheese, freshly grated

salt and pepper to season

1. Remove konjac rice from the package. Drain, rinse well, and then dry in paper towels. Set aside.
2. Heat olive oil in a large sauté pan over medium-high heat. Add the onion. Cook 2-3 minutes then add garlic.
3. Stir in konjac rice and cook about 2-3 minutes, then pour in wine and broth, stirring constantly. Cook until the liquid has mostly absorbed.
4. Add cream, tomato sauce, tomatoes, and salt and pepper.
5. When most of the cream has been absorbed, stir in parsley and lobster. Remove from heat
6. Finish the dish by stirring in butter, chives, and Parmesan.
7. Stir thoroughly until the ingredients are well mixed and the texture is thick and creamy. Adjust the seasoning.

Serve with the lobster tail atop the plate and a handful of freshly grated Parmesan and chives.

carbs	fibre	fat	protein
10g	4g	14g	23g

Our lobster roll salad can be added to any keto bun or bread, but is also super delicious in a lettuce wrap or just in a bowl with a spoon—your choice! We hope you enjoy our version.

Isn't it funny how your taste changes when you're keto? I was introduced to these rolls through a local fast-food joint. Every year I just couldn't wait 'til the summer promotion where they offered these to the masses. I kept thinking that I'd love to learn the secret to making these lobster rolls, but somehow never found the time.

Fast forward to current days and ketogenic living. We still love the lobster rolls, but these days our focus is more on making this recipe our own, where we can control the ingredients and explore our own flavour profiles.

LOBSTER ROLL

SERVINGS 4 **SERVING SIZE** ¼ of recipe

- 1 lobster, cooked and diced
- ½ cup celery, diced
- ½ cup mayo, or to taste
- 2 tbsp Dijon mustard
- 2 tbsp parsley, tarragon, basil leaves, or your favourite fresh herb, rough chopped
- 1 tbsp apple cider vinegar
- 2 tsp garlic powder
- salt and pepper, to taste
- diced avocado, diced tomatoes, diced cucumber, diced cheese (optional)

1. Combine all ingredients and adjust seasonings and mayo to your own taste.

carbs	fibre	fat	protein
4g	.5g	20g	10g

I've eaten a lot of scallops over the years; some of them were really good and others...well, not so much. Don't get me wrong, I still managed to eat the 'not so good' ones, but it sure gives you an appreciation for the finer details of how to cook a scallop.

The secret to the perfect seared scallop is making sure your pan is screaming hot before you add these delicate mollusks. This is a make-or-break dish; it's too easy to turn these delightful nuggets of protein into a ball of rubber that happens to taste like fish. So, take your time and pay attention to the details, and they will turn out meltingly good!

PAN-FRIED SCALLOPS *with* CELERIAC

SERVINGS 1 **SERVING SIZE** 5 scallops

5 scallops

2 tbsp oil

salt and pepper, to taste

curry powder, approximately ⅛ tsp per scallop

2 tbsp butter

celeriac root purée (optional)

1. Rinse scallops to remove any residual sand and then dry thoroughly with paper towels
2. Preheat a non-stick frying pan over medium-high heat.
3. Add the oil when the pan is hot; test by flicking some water into the oil. If the water sizzles, the oil is hot.
4. Place the scallops in the hot oil, making sure not to crowd the pan. If they are too close together the scallops will steam and be rubbery.
5. Once the scallops are in the pan, don't try to move them in any way; just allow them to cook for 2 minutes. During this time, season the top side of the scallop with salt, pepper, and a generous sprinkle of curry powder.
6. Add the butter to the pan in the last few seconds before flipping.
7. Flip the scallops. Cook for 1 more minute, while spooning butter over the scallops.
8. Remove the scallops from the pan and place on paper towels to drain excess oil, then serve.

Plate your scallops on individual beds of celeriac root purée as shown in our picture. Spoon or pipe a small dollop for every point where you will place a piece. This adds an ooey, gooey decadent layer and also makes your plate a little more satisfying/filling.

The added sprinkle of curry will elevate the dish without compromising the taste of the scallops.

carbs	fibre	fat	protein
3g	0g	25g	19g

This is a quick and easy salmon recipe that works as a weeknight family meal, but can also bring the oohs and aahs from company that you're trying to impress at a dinner party. You can even feel confident serving this one to the boss or the new in-laws!

SALMON *with* DIJON GLAZE

SERVINGS 4 **SERVING SIZE** 1 fillet

- 4-6 salmon fillets
- 2 garlic cloves, minced
- ¼ cup black olives, sliced
- ¼ cup Dijon mustard
- ¼ cup powdered sweetener
- ⅛ cup whole grain mustard
- 1 tbsp lemon juice
- 1 tbsp avocado oil
- 1 tsp parsley
- 1 tsp thyme
- 1 tsp Korean chili flakes
- ½ tsp onion powder or dry onion flakes

Himalayan pink or sea salt, and pepper, to taste

1. Preheat your oven to 375°F degrees.
2. Place the salmon on a parchment-lined baking sheet.
3. Mix together the remaining ingredients in a small bowl and generously coat the top of the salmon.
4. Bake the salmon for 18-20 minutes, depending on size of the fillets.

FOR A CEDAR PLANK ON THE GRILL

1. Soak cedar plank in salted water for 2 hours, then drain.
2. Lay the salmon on the plank and spread the sauce over the top and sides.
3. Set grill heat to medium-high. Place the cedar plank on the part of your grill away from the heat.
4. Put the cover down on your grill and cook for 20 to 30 minutes or until fish reaches an internal temperature of 135°F.
5. Serve tableside, right off the plank.

carbs	fibre	fat	protein
1.75g	0.25g	13g	5g

MEAT & POULTRY

Beef Burritos | 122

Cabbage Rolls | 124

Chicken Chimichangas | 126

Chicken Cordon Bleu | 128

Ginger Beef | 131

Homestyle Chicken Pot Pie | 132

Honey Garlic Spare Ribs | 135

Italian Crack Slaw | 136

Korean BBQ Chicken | 139

Mom's W Sauce Chops | 140

Pork Meatloaf with Asian Glaze | 143

Primavera Chicken with Tomato Sauce | 144

Roasted Rack of Lamb with White Balsamic Glaze | 147

Salisbury Steak with Mushroom Gravy | 148

Sloppy Joe Burger | 151

Southern-Fried Oven Chicken | 152

Sticky Kentucky Bourbon Chicken | 154

Sweet 'n' Sour Meatballs | 157

Veal Parmesan | 158

Vinegar Pork Chops | 161

All macro counts given are per serving.

Most of our friends know that hubby Geoff and I absolutely love to cook. On weekends we often start a big cook directly after eating breakfast, and then spend the whole day working together to prepare the biggest kind of scoff. We cook up everything from Asian, Mexican, Jamaican, and Indian, right on back to the traditional Newfoundland food that our grandparents made and passed down to us through our parents.

Geoff has been cooking this particular recipe since before our time together, but I've helped add to and enhance the original recipe, bringing it to a whole new level of yumminess. This Mexican shredded beef multitasks in many wonderful dishes in our home. Try it on your next plate of nachos instead of hamburger meat, add it to your favourite keto pizza, or add it to some baked cheese stacks for a wicked snack. Chimichangas or chili are other options for this shredded beef, and we've even stacked it on a keto bun with some nice sharp cheese and a little hot sauce for a quick and tasty sandwich lunch!

BEEF BURRITOS

SERVINGS 16 cups **SERVING SIZE** 1 cup

FOR THE BEEF

- 2 tbsp keto-friendly oil
- 5 lbs boneless beef roast—we usually do three small roasts for batch cooking
- 1 cup water
- 2 bay leaves
- 3 cups beef broth
- 1½ cups onion, finely chopped
- 1 can (28 oz) San Marzano crushed or diced tomatoes
- ⅓ cup chili powder
- 3 tbsp minced garlic
- 1 tbsp Korean chili flakes
- 3 tsp cumin
- 2 tsp oregano
- 2 tsp thyme
- 1 tsp Himalayan pink salt
- ½ tsp pepper
- ½ cup apple cider vinegar
- 1 can (7 oz) chopped green chiles

FOR THE WRAPS (PER INDIVIDUAL WRAP)

- wonton wrappers (see page 213 for recipe)
- 1 cup of Mexican shredded beef
- ⅛ cup cheese, grated—we use cheddar

note Nutrition is for the meat filling by itself, and does not include wrap or garnish.

carbs	fibre	fat	protein
6.4g	1.7g	20g	29g

FOR THE MEXICAN BEEF

1. In a large oven-safe pot or Dutch oven, add oil and beef and sear the meat on all sides to seal in flavour.
2. Add water and bay leaves. Bring to a boil, then reduce heat to medium-low.
3. Cover and simmer for 30 minutes, turning meat twice.
4. While simmering, add in broth, onions, tomatoes, and spices.
5. Cover and place in preheated 300°F oven for 1½ to 2 hours depending on the size of the roast. Turn meat at ½-hour intervals.
6. Add vinegar after 1 hour and top up broth if needed.
7. Cover and return to the oven for at least another hour, turning again halfway through.
8. Remove pot from the oven and discard bay leaves; at this point the beef should be tender and easy to pull apart. Let meat cool enough to handle.
9. Remove beef to a cutting board and reserve pan juices.
10. While meat is cooling, add green chiles to the pan.

11. Bring the pan juices to a boil for 15-20 minutes to reduce the sauce, stirring often. Sauce will be done when it's reduced by about half.
12. Using your fingers or two forks, pull the meat apart into a bite-sized shred. We like to chop against the grain first, to ensure there will be no really long strands.
13. Add pulled meat back to the reduced sauce. Stir until evenly mixed. Set aside.
14. Preheat oven to 350°F.

PUTTING IT TOGETHER

1. Roll out the wonton wrappers between two sheets of parchment paper, making sure the rolled out/flattened dough is larger than the size you want your finished wrapper. Use a pot lid as a cookie cutter to make your perfectly shaped round wrap.
2. Spread the beef in a thin line down the centre of the wrap and cover with cheese. Close the wrap by rolling it up, then place it on a parchment-covered baking sheet with the seam side down. Sprinkle more cheese on top of the wrap.
3. Bake for 20 minutes, until the cheese is melted, wrap has slightly crisped, and the meat is heated throughout.
4. Let cool slightly and garnish as desired. We suggest sour cream, shredded cheese, diced tomatoes, shredded lettuce, and Saucy Salsa (see page 244 in our first book for recipe).

15 cabbage leaves

FOR THE MEAT FILLING

- 2 tbsp olive oil
- 1 medium onion, chopped
- 3 cloves of garlic, minced
- 1 tbsp parsley
- 1 tsp oregano
- 1 tsp thyme
- ⅓ tsp basil

Himalayan pink salt, and pepper, to taste

- 1 lb ground beef
- 1 package shirataki rice
- ½ can (28 oz) tomatoes, crushed or chopped; reserve second half for use in sauce

FOR THE SAUCE

- 2 tbsp olive oil
- ½ onion, chopped
- 4 cloves garlic, minced
- 1½ cans (28 oz can) crushed tomato
- 1 can (680ml/24 fluid oz approximately) tomato sauce
- 1 cup water
- ¼ cup apple cider vinegar
- 3 tbsp coconut sauce
- 2 tbsp powdered sweetener
- 1 tsp oregano
- 1 tsp parsley
- ½ tsp thyme
- ⅛ tsp nutmeg

Himalayan pink salt, and pepper, to taste

carbs	fibre	fat	protein
13g	5g	8g	10g

Out of all the dishes that I have ketofied and created since starting this keto way of eating, none of them have given me the level of satisfaction that came from transforming cabbage rolls. I have always loved cabbage rolls. I have very fond memories of watching my mother make them and it was a foregone conclusion that I would eventually try my hand at ketofying them.

Making rice-less cabbage rolls just seemed like meatballs covered in cabbage. It was missing the rice component in this traditional dish and while we don't eat regular rice, there is no reason we can't deck our rolls out with shirataki rice! After a few unsuccessful attempts, we knew we had finally mastered the creation! I can promise you, there will always be a batch of these put aside in our freezer for quick weeknight meals. It's on the top of the list for our all-time favourite foods.

CABBAGE ROLLS

SERVINGS 15 cups **SERVING SIZE** 1 cabbage roll

1. Blanch large cabbage leaves in a large pot of boiling water for 3-5 minutes to soften them.

   note Don't overcook the leaves or they will break apart when you're rolling them.

2. Set aside to cool.

to remove the leaves from head of cabbage, cut approximately ¼" off the stump/bottom of the head and place the whole head of cabbage in boiling water. Boil for about 2 minutes. Peel off the softened leaves. Place remaining head back in the boiling water and repeat until all of the leaves are removed. Remove any tough stems from cooked leaves.

If you have some smaller leaves and still have filling leftover, you can overlap the leaves as needed to form sheets of cabbage. The rolls will still cook up perfectly.

FOR THE MEAT MIXTURE

1. Place oil and onion in a sauté pan and cook over medium heat for about 3 minutes, until the onion turns translucent. Add garlic and continue to cook for 2 more minutes.
2. Turn off heat and mix in parsley, oregano, thyme, basil, salt, and pepper.
3. Transfer onion mixture to a large bowl. Set aside to cool.
4. Add uncooked ground beef, ½ can tomatoes, and shirataki rice to the cooled onion mix.

   note **Don't overwork the meat or compress it too much or it will result in a tough cabbage roll.**
5. Set aside.

FOR THE SAUCE

1. Place oil and onion in a sauté pan and cook over medium heat for about 3 minutes, or until the onion starts to turn translucent.
2. Add garlic and continue to cook for 2 more minutes.
3. Add remaining ingredients and simmer for 5-10 minutes. Set aside to cool.

PUTTING IT TOGETHER

1. Preheat oven to 350°F.
2. Spread a thin layer of sauce on the bottom of a large baking dish.
3. Cut the thick end of the stem off of the cabbage leaves with a knife. Our leaves were extra big, so we cut them right in half, directly along the spine of the leaf, making two out of one.
4. Place about ⅓ cup meat mixture into one end of each leaf on a diagonal, about 1 inch from the edge of the cabbage leaf. Then roll the leaf, tucking in the sides as you roll. Place the finished rolls seam-side down on top of sauce in baking dish.
5. Repeat process for all cabbage leaves.
6. Spoon remaining sauce on top of cabbage rolls, then cover. Bake 1 hour 15 minutes, topping up liquids as needed, until rice and meat are cooked through.

Add extra water or sauce to the pan as needed to keep the dish sauced and to prevent the cabbage rolls from drying out.

2 tbsp keto oil

4 chicken breasts, boneless and skinless

1 onion, diced

3 cloves garlic, minced

1 jalapeño pepper (or ¼ cup bell peppers), with seeds and ribs removed, diced

1½ tsp chili powder

½ tsp cumin

¼ tsp cinnamon

⅛ tsp nutmeg

Himalayan pink salt, and pepper, to taste

1 small tomato, chopped

¼ cup olives, minced

2 tbsp fresh cilantro, chopped (optional)

¼ cup apple cider vinegar

¼ cup powdered sweetener

FOR THE SAUCE

1 tbsp olive oil

½ cup onion, diced

2 garlic cloves, minced

1 tsp chili powder

½ tsp cumin

½ tsp smoked paprika

1 can (4 oz) chopped green chiles, drained and rinsed (optional)

½ cup chicken broth

½ cup tomato sauce

Three 10-inch keto wraps (see recipe page 213)

1 cup cheddar cheese, shredded

carbs	fibre	fat	protein
13g	3g	32g	18g

Chimichangas are traditionally deep-fried wraps full of meat and spices. The one thing I've learned throughout my keto journey is to keep it simple! It's hard enough getting that wrap recipe just right and then getting it perfectly formed when you're using keto ingredients. Deep frying would just add another step of worry to getting this recipe just right. So, our chimichangas are baked in the oven after being coated with a mix of butter and oil.

I experienced my first chimichanga while visiting Ottawa, years ago. The little restaurant was overlooking the Rideau canal, where we watched all the skaters enjoying the natural ice while we ate. They sure looked cold out there, but I was toasty warm inside with a tummy full of chicken and spices. That meal became one of my food memories for that trip. I fell in love with the crispy wrap, the spiced chicken and the melty cheese in every bite! So, I knew it would be recreated in our own kitchen someday, with my own favourite blend of spices.

CHICKEN CHIMICHANGAS

SERVINGS 3 **SERVING SIZE** 1 chimichanga

FOR THE WRAPS

1. Preheat the oven to 350°F and prepare a baking sheet with foil and parchment paper.
2. Heat the oil in a large sauté or frying pan.
3. Add chicken to the pan and sauté over medium heat until cooked through, about 12-15 minutes.
4. Remove chicken from pan and set aside to cool.
5. Add the onion and cook until translucent, about 5 minutes.
6. Add garlic and pepper and cook until soft, about 3 minutes.
7. Add the spices and continue to cook for 30 seconds.
8. Add the tomato, olives, and cilantro and cook for about 2 minutes.

note Macros do not include wraps.

9. Deglaze pan with ¼ cup of apple cider vinegar.
10. Meanwhile, shred your chicken or cut it into thin strips.
11. Stir the chicken back into the pan, add sweetener, and continue to cook for 10 minutes.
12. Remove pan from stove and transfer chicken mix to a bowl, reserving ¼ of the mix as starter for your sauce.

FOR THE SAUCE

1. Add oil to the sauté pan with your reserved chicken mix.
2. Sauté onion for about 5 minutes.
3. Add garlic and cook for 3 minutes.
4. Add spices and continue to cook for 30 seconds to a minute.
5. Stir in green chiles and cook for 2 minutes.
6. Add chicken broth and tomato sauce and simmer until thickened; purée if desired, but we like the sauce on the rustic/chunkier side.

   Note **Use extra water to thin out your sauce if it is thicker than you like.**

PUTTING IT TOGETHER

1. Place a wrap on a sheet of parchment.
2. Spread 1 cup chicken mixture in a strip down the centre of each keto-friendly wrap, leaving a 2-inch edge on both ends that has no chicken. This is where you will fold your wrap into itself to form the packets.
3. Place ¼ cup cheese on top of the chicken mix.
4. Fold in the two empty sides back over the cheese and chicken, then roll in the top and bottom edges.
5. Put the wraps seam-side down on the prepared baking sheet.
6. Brush the top of the wrap with butter-oil mixture.
7. Bake 8 to 10 minutes per side, brushing again after you flip them.

FOR BRUSHING

2 tbsp butter, melted

2 tbsp olive oil or keto equivalent

The French term *cordon bleu* translates into blue ribbon, and was originally an award that was given to women cooks for their culinary excellence. The use of the term has loosened over the years and is more recently applied to any superior cook. It's also the name of this dish.

The classic Chicken Cordon Bleu is coated in a flour and spice mixture; in our keto version, we use those same spices inside the roll. Instead of the breading, we cover ours with bacon. If you would rather the breading, use the breading from our Southern-Fried Oven Chicken, found on page 152. It's an easy swap-out.

We hope you and your family enjoy this simple recipe.

CHICKEN CORDON BLEU

SERVINGS 4 **SERVING SIZE** 1

- 4 chicken breasts, boneless and skinless
- 1 tbsp smoked paprika
- ½ tsp Himalayan pink salt
- ½ tsp garlic powder
- ½ tsp onion powder
- ½ tsp thyme
- ¼ tsp pepper
- ¼ tsp oregano
- ½ lb ham, thinly sliced
- 6 oz Swiss, provolone, gruyère or other mild cheese

FOR THE BACON WRAP

- 8 pieces of bacon, uncooked

1. Preheat oven to 350°F.
2. Place the chicken between 2 sheets of plastic wrap; this will protect your kitchen from splattered raw chicken juice as you flatten the chicken.
3. Pound the chicken with a meat mallet or rolling pin until it is ¼-inch thick. If the chicken breast is really thick, you can butterfly it open before pounding.
4. Mix dry ingredients together and sprinkle the spice mix over the top of the flattened chicken.
5. Place ham and cheese in the centre of each chicken breast and roll up the chicken so it resembles a jelly roll.
6. Wrap each chicken breast in 2 slices of bacon. Place the chicken breasts, bacon-seam-side-down on a parchment-covered baking sheet.
7. Bake for 30-45 minutes or until bacon is crisp and chicken is cooked through, basting the chicken occasionally with the pan drippings. Use additional time if the bacon is not crisp.

carbs	fibre	fat	protein
1.2g	0.2g	30g	46g

Since ovens are all different and chicken breasts can vary in size, bake times will vary. The bacon should be crispy! If you prefer extra crispy bacon, broil for an additional 1-2 minutes.

This dish boasts deep and unctuous flavours that are spiced to perfection. Serve this alongside a small serving of cauliflower rice, some shirataki noodles, or just by itself. There is enough flavour in this dish for it to stand alone.

Geoff likes to stir this all together on his plate, while I like the individual taste each component offers to the dish, so I just let the meat/sauce sit on top of the veggies. Either way you choose to serve this up, it's gonna become a new family favourite.

GINGER BEEF

SERVINGS 8 **SERVING SIZE** 1 cup

FOR THE MARINADE

¼ cup coconut sauce

1 lb beef, thinly sliced

1 tsp garlic powder

1 tsp ginger powder

salt and pepper—we use 1 tsp salt and ½ tsp pepper

FOR THE STIR-FRY

2 tbsp olive oil

1 medium onion, diced

3 cloves of garlic, minced

2 tbsp ginger, finely chopped

2 cups broccoli, thinly sliced

1 cup mushrooms, thinly sliced

1 cup bell peppers, thinly sliced

½ cups carrots, julienned (optional)

2 tbsp coconut sauce

1 tsp red pepper flakes or Korean chili flakes

1 tsp Himalayan pink or sea salt

½ tsp pepper

½ tsp cumin

½ cups beef broth

¼ cup apple cider vinegar

1 tbsp sesame seeds, to garnish

¼ cup green onions, diced, to garnish

1. Place all marinade ingredients in a bowl and let sit while you prep your other ingredients. Make sure all the meat is covered.
2. Add oil and onion to a large sauté pan and cook over medium heat until translucent.
3. Add sliced meat from the marinade (reserve marinade for later in the recipe) and cook for about 3-5 minutes, depending on how thick you sliced your beef. Beef will get tough if overcooked.
4. Remove onions and beef from the pan and set aside.
5. Add remaining marinade, garlic, ginger, broccoli, mushrooms, peppers, carrots, coconut sauce, spices, and broth to the pan and cook for about 5 minutes, or until the mushrooms and broccoli are cooked through.

   note **Do not re-use the marinade bowl unless it has been cleaned after meat has marinated.**
6. Remove veggies from pan and place them in a deep bowl.
7. Deglaze pan with vinegar to get all the good pan drippings. Reduce the vinegar by about two-thirds and then pour the pan drippings over the veggies. Stir to combine.
8. Plate your veggies in individual bowls and add the previously cooked beef to the top of the bowls, garnish and serve.

Xanthan gum can be sprinkled in if you would like a thicker sauce, but our preference is to just reduce the sauce to our liking by cooking for a longer period of time.

carbs	fibre	fat	protein
10g	2g	7g	14g

Nothing beats the comfort of a chicken pot pie. This recipe is full of velvety broth, juicy bits of chicken and lots of keto-friendly veggies. The celeriac makes a great potato substitute; with only 5.9 carbs and 1.2 fibre per 100g, it comes in at almost five times less that the spuds we used to put in our stews. It also has the advantage that it freezes well, so you can make a batch of this stew and store it away for a fast and easy supper down the road.

This pie can be done with a top and/or bottom crust, but our preference is to just use the top layer. This is also easier as you don't have to pre-bake the bottom crust; just make your chicken filling, add the top crust and pop it in the oven. This is a delightful and delicious chicken pot pie that will satisfy your family's cravings, with or without the crust.

HOMESTYLE CHICKEN POT PIE

SERVINGS 6 **SERVING SIZE** 1 cup

FOR THE CRUST

- 1 cup almond flour
- ¼ cup coconut flour
- ¼ tsp Himalayan pink or sea salt
- ½ tsp Xanthan gum
- ½ cup butter, cold, cut into chunks
- 2 tbsp vinegar

coconut flour, for dusting the parchment (if needed)

FOR THE STEW

- 2 tbsp olive oil
- 3 chicken breasts, chopped into 1-inch pieces
- 1 medium onion, diced
- 3 cloves garlic, minced
- 1 tsp Himalayan pink salt
- 1 tsp thyme
- 1 tsp parsley
- ½ tsp pepper
- ½ tsp coriander
- 3 cups chicken or veggie broth
- 1½ cups celeriac, diced into ¾-inch cubes
- 3 carrots, sliced
- ¾ cup mushrooms, sliced
- ¼ cup green beans, cut into 1-inch pieces
- ¼ cup apple cider vinegar
- ¼ to ½ tsp Xanthan gum

carbs	fibre	fat	protein
15.5g	5.9g	16g	18g

FOR THE CRUST

1. Mix together all dry ingredients with a whisk.
2. Add butter chunks and use a pastry cutter to incorporate the butter into the dry ingredients. At this stage the dough will resemble a damp, coarse sand.
3. Place dough in the fridge to cool for 15 minutes.

   note **A food processor can be used instead of a pastry cutter. Pulse to combine until crumbly, then add vinegar and pulse again. Dough will be crumbly when finished. Continue with step 4.**

4. When cooled, remove dough from fridge and sprinkle the vinegar over the top. With your hands, work the vinegar into the dough. Keep in mind that the more you press the dough the tougher it will be, so make sure to use a light hand.
5. Form the dough into a ball and refrigerate for another 15 minutes to let the ingredients come together.

Heat from your hands will melt the butter in your pastry before it's supposed to! Use a pastry cutter as much as possible.

FOR THE STEW

1. Add the oil, chicken and onion to a large, oven-safe pot and cook over medium heat until chicken is cooked through, about 8-10 minutes. Stir often to make sure it doesn't catch on the pan.
2. Remove the chicken and set aside.
3. Add garlic and spices and cook for 5 minutes.
4. Add broth, then turn heat down to a simmer. Add celeriac and carrot.
5. Simmer for 10 minutes or until veggies are cooked through.
6. Add mushrooms and green beans and continue to cook for 10 minutes.
7. Add the vinegar and cover. Simmer for about 10 minutes.
8. Sprinkle on Xanthan gum and whisk to incorporate.

note We use a shaker to sprinkle in a bit at a time to reach our desired thickness for the stew. It needs to be thick enough to support the top crust.

9. Set stew aside to cool.

PUTTING IT TOGETHER

1. Preheat over to 300°F.
2. Roll dough out between two sheets of parchment paper.
3. Place crust on top of the cooled stew. Double up the crust on the outside edges to create a thicker edge. Using your finger and thumb, pinch the crust to create a scalloped pattern all the way around the edge.
4. Place chicken pie in the preheated oven and cook until the top is slightly golden, about 20 minutes. We placed a cookie sheet below ours to catch any spill-overs.

Cover edges of the pie crust with foil if the outer edges start to burn.

If you're doing a bottom crust, press the dough into a baking dish and bake at 350°F for 15-20 minutes, or until the crust is a light golden brown. Let it cool completely before adding your stew.

In the early days of a ketogenic lifestyle, your head is spinning with all the things you think you'll never eat again. Honey garlic was one of those foods for me, as we don't eat honey. How are we supposed to have honey garlic without honey? When you're further along in your keto journey you start to get creative. The honey was easily swapped out for some keto-friendly sweetener. All we had to do was add in our own flavour profile and we'd be all set.

These ribs will be the type you're used to having at a Chinese restaurant, packed with garlic, sweetness, and full-on flavour. With any luck, our honey garlic recipe will relieve the worry that you'll never eat this delicious meal again.

HONEY GARLIC SPARE RIBS

SERVINGS 4 **SERVING SIZE** ¼ of ribs

2 to 3 lbs of pork side ribs, individual short cut

- 8 cloves garlic, minced
- 2 cups broth
- ½ cup powdered sweetener
- ⅓ cup apple cider vinegar
- ¼ cup coconut sauce
- 2 tsp Himalayan pink salt
- 1 tsp coriander
- 1 tsp Korean chili flakes
- 1 tsp smoked paprika
- 1 tsp fresh ginger, grated or minced

TO FINISH

- ½ tsp garlic powder
- ⅓ tsp parsley

1. Preheat oven to 325°F.
2. Cut ribs between each bone for single-bone pieces.
3. Place ribs in a roaster; add remaining ingredients to a bullet or blender, and combine as a sauce. Pour over ribs in the roasting pan.
4. Cover and bake for 3 hours. Check every 60 minutes to stir and make sure there's still liquid at the bottom. Top up with water and/or broth as needed.
5. Increase oven temperature to 375°F and cook for 20 minutes uncovered
6. Just before you take the ribs out, turn the oven on broil and broil for no more than a couple of minutes. Keep an eye on them to make sure they only start to caramelize a little and not burn.
7. Remove roaster from the oven and transfer to stovetop.
8. Remove the ribs from the sauce and set ribs aside.
9. Turn stovetop to medium-high and add ½ tsp garlic powder to the pan juices.
10. Continue to cook on stovetop to reduce the sauce to your preferred thickness. *note* **¼ tsp Xanthan gum may be sprinkled in to thicken, if needed.**
11. Add ribs back to pot, stir and sprinkle parsley for garnish, then serve.

carbs	fibre	fat	protein
7.2g	0.5g	58g	43g

- ½ lb hamburger meat, or alternate minced meat
- Himalayan pink salt, and pepper, to taste
- ½ medium onion, diced
- 2 cloves garlic, minced
- 14 oz cabbage, sliced and roughly chopped
- ½ cup water
- 1½ tsp oregano
- 1 tsp thyme
- 1 tsp onion powder
- ½ tsp basil
- ½ tsp rosemary
- ½ tsp sage
- ½ tsp Korean chili flakes
- ½ tsp coriander
- ½ tsp chili
- 1 tbsp coconut sauce
- 1 tbsp hot sauce
- 5-6 mushrooms, sliced thick
- 1 tsp ginger, grated
- ¼ cup apple cider vinegar
- 1 cup tomato sauce
- 6-8 baby tomatoes, halved

carbs	fibre	fat	protein
11g	3g	11g	13g

I think if Geoff could have his own way, we would eat crack slaw six out of seven nights of the week. If it wasn't for his love of steak to break it up, it would be the full seven nights!

Because we have this so often it's important (for me, anyway) to switch it up with different flavours, and luckily crack slaw is one of those recipes that can be tweaked for any flavour profile. This is our Italian version; no side dish needed.

ITALIAN CRACK SLAW

SERVINGS 4 **SERVING SIZE** 1½ cups

1. Brown ground beef and season with salt and pepper to taste. We used 1 tsp salt and ½ tsp pepper. Remove from pan and set aside.
2. In the same pan, sauté onions and garlic for 5 minutes or until onions are translucent.
3. Push onion and garlic back to the sides of the pan and add spices directly into the fat. This will help the spices bloom.
4. Add cabbage, water, and spices. Cover to steam the cabbage until wilted, stirring occasionally so it is mixed through and cooks evenly.
5. Stir in the coconut sauce, hot sauce, mushrooms, and ginger.
6. Deglaze pan with vinegar. Use a wooden spoon to get the browned bits off the bottom of the pan.
7. Return the hamburger to the pan, and add tomatoes. Mix well and continue cooking for 5-10 minutes; adjust liquid level to your own liking, adding extra water if you like a thinner sauce.
8. Serve with extra hot sauce on the side for added heat. Enjoy!

Add extra water to the pot as you sauté the cabbage, if needed.

SEASONING BLENDS

Love this Italian crack slaw, but want to change this recipe up and make it brand new again? Try these spice blends for alternate cuisines! Swap out the Italian spices in the recipe for any of these, or make up your own!

MEXICAN BLEND

2 tsp chili powder
2 tsp garlic powder
1 tsp onion powder
½ tsp crushed red pepper flakes
¼ tsp dried oregano
2 tsp smoked paprika
1½ tsp ground cumin
½ tsp Himalayan pink salt
½ tsp black pepper
pinch cinnamon
pinch cloves

CURRY BLEND

2 tbsp coriander
2 tbsp cumin
2 tbsp ground ginger
1½ tbsp turmeric
1 tsp dry mustard
1 tsp Himalayan pink salt
1 tsp cinnamon
½ tsp pepper
½ tsp cardamom
½ tsp cayenne pepper

In the early days of the East Coast Keto Test Kitchen, it was a bit of a challenge getting our grown son to eat our meals. At the time he didn't have a good understanding of what keto meant and was a little apprehensive about trying our improved recipes. After one such conversation about the health benefits of keto, he had one simple request: "Do you know what would be cool, Mudder? If you could make me some Korean BBQ Chicken. I would love that!"

You got it, kiddo! We set right to work! After a few attempts, it was perfected and he was delighted with the end result. My son would tell you that the veggies are optional. Include them if you wish.

KOREAN BBQ CHICKEN

SERVINGS 4 **SERVING SIZE** 2 chicken thighs and sauce

FOR THE MARINADE

- ¼ cup apple cider vinegar
- 3 cloves garlic, minced
- 3 tbsp coconut sauce
- 2 tbsp powdered sweetener
- 2 tsp ginger, finely grated with a microplane
- 2 tsp Korean chili flakes or roasted red pepper flakes
- 1 tsp Himalayan pink salt
- ½ tsp pepper

FOR THE CHICKEN

- 8 chicken thighs, boneless, skinless, cut into 1-inch cubes
- 2 tbsp oil
- ⅓ cup onion, finely chopped
- mushrooms, roughly chopped
- peppers, roughly chopped

1. Combine all the marinade ingredients in a glass bowl and then add chicken. Stir to ensure the chicken is thoroughly coated with marinade.

   note **Tough cuts of beef may benefit from lengthy marination, but chicken does best with short soaks. Any longer may have the opposite effect and toughen the chicken. Marinate for no more than 2 hours.**

2. Refrigerate for 30 minutes to 2 hours.
3. Add oil and onion to a preheated sauté pan.
4. Add chicken and marinade to pan. Cook for 8-10 minutes, stirring to ensure the meat is cooking on all sides.
5. Add veggies and continue to cook until the chicken and veggies are cooked through.

Use a microplane—a type of fine grater—to grate the ginger.

carbs	fibre	fat	protein
8g	1.25g	28g	34g

If using daikon, we recommend parboiling them before adding to the pan, to help with the cook time.

Mom's Worcestershire sauce chops were the best! While mom's food was always yummy, this dish was one to look forward to. Hers were traditionally cooked and served with sliced potatoes in the same pan, but we prefer ours with just meat, sauce, and green veggies on the side. If you would like that white side, add some super thin slices of daikon or chayote squash when you add the braising liquid. Spoon some of the liquid over the top and cover.

Mom used full-octane Worcestershire sauce back in the day, but as that's full of wheat it's a keto no-go. Our keto-friendly version uses coconut sauce instead.

MOM'S W SAUCE PORK CHOPS

SERVINGS 2 **SERVING SIZE** 1 pork chop and half the sauce

- 2 tbsp keto-friendly oil
- 2 pork chops
- 1 medium onion, sliced
- ¼ cup coconut sauce
- 3 cloves garlic, minced
- 1 tbsp fish sauce
- 1 tsp Korean chili flakes
- 1 tsp thyme
- 1 tsp turmeric
- 1 tsp Himalayan pink salt
- ½ tsp pepper
- ½ cup broth or water
- 6 mushrooms, sliced
- 9 baby tomatoes

1. Remove chops from the fridge beforehand so that they come to room temperature.
2. Add oil to a large-size sauté pan over medium-high heat.
3. When pan is hot, add pork chops and onion. Sear both sides of the meat until the outside of the chops are brown, about 2-3 minutes per side.
4. Add remaining ingredients except mushroom and tomatoes and then cover and reduce heat to low.
5. Cook for 45 minutes to 1 hour, or until pork chops become tender.
6. Add mushrooms and tomato to the pan and cook through, topping up liquid as needed.
7. Remove pork and allow it to rest for at least 5 minutes, to keep the meat tender.
8. Reduce sauce in the pan over medium heat while the chops are resting.
9. Spoon sauce over chops after plating them.

carbs	fibre	fat	protein
17g	5g	27g	43g

If you prefer to finish in the oven, after searing the meat cover your oven-safe skillet with a lid or foil. Cook in a preheated 325°F oven for about 45 to 55 minutes, or until tender.

This is a perfectly seasoned meatloaf with an exceptionally delicious glaze. Serve with a small serving of celeriac purée, or cauliflower and a steamed green vegetable topped with butter. We think you're gonna absolutely love this recipe; it's the perfect family meal!

Ground turkey or chicken can be substituted for pork.

PORK MEATLOAF *with* ASIAN GLAZE

SERVINGS 6 **SERVING SIZE** ⅙ of the recipe

FOR THE MEATLOAF

- 2 tbsp oil
- 1 medium onion, diced
- 1 carrot, grated
- 2 cloves garlic, minced
- 2 lbs ground pork
- ⅓ cup almond flour or crushed pork rinds
- 1 egg
- 2 tbsp fresh ginger, grated
- 1 tbsp fish sauce
- 1 tsp salt
- ½ tsp pepper

FOR THE SPICY GLAZE

- ½ cup tomato sauce
- ¼ cup coconut sauce
- ¼ cup broth
- 1 tsp red curry paste
- 1 tsp ginger, grated
- 1 tsp salt
- ½ tsp pepper
- ¼ tsp turmeric
- ⅛ tsp cardamom
- ⅛ tsp garam masala

small bunch green onions or chives, chopped, to garnish

1. Preheat oven to 450°F.
2. In a small sauté pan over medium heat, add oil and onion and sauté for 3-5 minutes, until onion starts to turn translucent.
3. Add carrot and garlic. Sauté for 2 more minutes then remove from heat to cool.
4. In a large bowl, add the pork, almond flour or pork rinds, onion mix, egg, ginger, fish sauce, and spices. Using your hands, gently combine.

   note **The more pressure you use here, the tougher the meatloaf. Use a gentle hand.**
5. Transfer the meat mixture to a foil or parchment-paper-lined baking sheet. Shape the mixture into two tightly-packed loaves, about 7 inches by 2 inches, or you can use a loaf pan.
6. In a small bowl, combine glaze ingredients; add to saucepan and simmer for 10-12 minutes.
7. Bake the meatloaf for 25-30 minutes and then remove from the oven. Pour off any excess fat and add about ¼ of the glaze to the top of the meatloaf.
8. Return to the oven and cook for another 10-15 minutes, or until meatloaf is cooked through.
9. Let rest at least 5 minutes before cutting.
10. Plate the meatloaf with a drizzle of the remaining glaze. Garnish with the sliced green tops of the green onions, or with chives.

This recipe also makes great meatballs and sauce. Or try the meatloaf cold on a piece of keto toast as a sandwich! Delightful!

carbs	fibre	fat	protein
9.5g	1.1g	39g	29g

Primavera was one of my favourite dishes from long ago. Primavera means 'Springtime' in Italian, so a primavera recipe in the culinary world means the best and brightest of spring vegetables on a plate. All those veggies combined with herbs and spices—how could anyone resist?

A traditional primavera is a pasta dish made with lightly sautéed spring vegetables. Ours can be served with celeriac purée, konjac noodles, or spiralized zoodles, but we prefer it just as is, spooned up from a bowl.

PRIMAVERA CHICKEN *with* TOMATO SAUCE

SERVINGS 2 **SERVING SIZE** half the recipe

- 2 tbsp keto-friendly oil
- ½ medium-size onion, roughly diced
- 2 chicken breasts, boneless and skinless, sliced into strips roughly ½ inch thick
- ⅓ bell pepper, sliced into strips
- 4-6 fresh mushrooms, sliced thick
- 1 tsp oregano
- ½ tsp basil
- ½ tsp thyme
- ½ tsp Korean chili flakes
- ¼ cup apple cider vinegar
- ½ can (28 oz can) of tomatoes with liquid, cut into bite-size chunks
- ½ cup fresh spinach
- salt and pepper, to taste
- grated Parmesan cheese, to garnish

1. Add oil, onion, and chicken to a large sauté pan and cook over medium heat.
2. Add peppers, mushrooms, and spices after about 5 minutes and continue to cook until the peppers are soft and the chicken is cooked through, about 8-10 minutes.
3. Deglaze the pan with vinegar, making sure to scrape off the brown bits at the bottom of the pan.
4. Stir in tomatoes and spinach, then reduce heat to a simmer. Simmer for 5 minutes until the tomatoes are warm.
5. Remove from heat and either grate Parmesan over the pan, if you're serving family style, or plate individually and sprinkle cheese atop each plate.

carbs	fibre	fat	protein
14.5g	3.5g	15g	15g

Make sure to add lots of grated Parmesan to the top; it adds saltiness, lends a cheesy layer, and also helps with the presentation of the dish.

This rack of lamb is a delicate and light offering for the dinner table. It does best at a medium-rare, but we've included the temperatures for a longer cook if desired.

The balsamic glaze should be done with a white balsamic vinegar, as the dark-coloured vinegars are loaded with added sugars. The finished glaze can be drizzled on top of the plated chops or you can finish the chops in the glaze in the pan, and serve them smothered in sauce. These go wonderfully with a small serving of celeriac purée and a roasted green veggie.

ROASTED RACK OF LAMB *with* WHITE BALSAMIC GLAZE

SERVINGS 4 **SERVING SIZE** 1 double chop of lamb, with sauce

FOR THE RUB

¼ cup onion, minced

⅓ cup white balsamic vinegar

2 tbsp olive oil

½ tsp thyme

½ tsp oregano

¼ tsp basil

salt and pepper, to taste

FOR THE MEAT

1 rack of lamb, to be cut into 4 double chops

salt and pepper, to season

2 tbsp oil

1. Combine all rub ingredients and set aside.
2. Preheat oven to 325°F.
3. Season meat with salt and pepper.
4. Heat oil in an oven-safe heavy frying pan over high heat, until hot.
5. Add lamb rack to the hot pan and using a pair of tongs, brown the meat on all sides, about 2-3 minutes per side.
6. Remove from heat and coat the meat in the pan with the herb mixture.
7. Cover the exposed bone ends with tin foil and place in oven; roast until thermometer inserted diagonally into centre of meat registers as follows:

   MEDIUM-RARE 145°F **MEDIUM** 160°F **WELL DONE** 170°F
8. Remove the rack of lamb to a plate or rack and reserve pan juices. Let the meat rest for 10 minutes.
9. Put the pan back on the stovetop and turn heat to medium-high to thicken the glaze.
10. Cook until the sauce has reduced by half and thickened slightly.

    note **Xanthan gum may be used to further thicken the sauce if needed.**
11. After resting, cut each rack into 4 double chops.

carbs	fibre	fat	protein
2.5g	.25g	30g	25g

Hubby loves keto burgers, and likes to eat them often. As much as I love an occasional patty on the grill, I'm a person who needs food variety. So, every now and then when he wants burgers and I don't want to fuss with making an extra meal, I switch it up and turn my own burger into Salisbury steak with a rich, thick, mushroom gravy.

We don't add extras to our burgers, as great burgers only need salt and pepper, but we add a little extra to the Salisbury steaks. Feel free to tweak the spices to make it your own.

SALISBURY STEAK *with* MUSHROOM GRAVY

SERVINGS 6 **SERVING SIZE** ⅓ lb patty and sauce

FOR THE SALISBURY STEAK

- 2 lb ground meat
- 1 tbsp dried onion flakes
- 1 tsp Himalayan pink salt
- ½ tsp garlic powder
- ½ tsp pepper
- 1 medium onion, halved and sliced

FOR THE GRAVY

- ¼ cup apple cider vinegar
- 2 tbsp butter
- 2 cups button mushrooms, sliced
- ⅛ cup coconut sauce
- ½ cup beef broth
- ½ tsp thyme
- ½ tsp Korean chili flakes
- ½ tsp garlic powder
- salt and pepper, to taste
- ⅛ to ¼ tsp Xanthan gum

note Macros are based on ⅓ lb of meat per person.

carbs	fibre	fat	protein
4.5g	0.7g	33g	30g

FOR THE SALISBURY STEAK

1. Combine all ingredients except onion, and form meat into oval patties, about 1 inch thick, and use your thumb to press an indent in the centre of each, creating a well. This allows the patty to cook evenly throughout.
2. Add oil to a heated sauté pan; add your patties and place your onions all around the patties.
3. Cook your burgers to your preferred doneness, making sure to keep moving your onions so they cook evenly. Remove patties.

FOR THE GRAVY

1. In the same pan you used to cook your patties, add apple cider vinegar to deglaze the pan, stirring to scrape any bits off the bottom of the pan.
2. Melt the butter and add the mushrooms. Cook on medium, for about 3 minutes per side.
3. Add the coconut sauce, broth, and spices; stir and cook for 3 minutes.
4. Sprinkle in Xanthan gum or cook the gravy on low for an extra 5 minutes to thicken it.

Add extra broth or water for more gravy.

Approximate cook times for cooking 1-inch burgers in a skillet on medium-high heat are as follows:

MEDIUM-RARE	130-135°F (red in the middle) 6 minutes total, or 3 mins per side
MEDIUM	145°F (pink in the middle) 7-8 minutes total or 4 mins per side
MEDIUM-WELL DONE	150-155°F (trace of pink in the middle) 9 minutes total or 4.5 mins per side
WELL DONE	160-165°F (no pink) 10 minutes total or 5 mins per side

I've always loved this piled-high, spicy, and sloppy cousin to the burger, but Geoff is a little different. While he describes me as 'wild as a baby goat,' he is a little more refined and likes everything in its place. So 'sloppy' doesn't cut it for him. It's just so...well, messy.

Unwiches and 'bunless' burgers have been a game-changer for him. It allows him to put the fixin's on a plate and just spoon them up as is; no worrying about the messy business of making sure you keep your shirt front clean. Me? Baby goat suits me just fine, so if you see me with a little tomato sauce on my pretty blouse, don't feel badly for me. Rest assured that I just demolished a wicked ol' Sloppy Joe burger and loved every second of it!

Whether you're wild and woolly, or tidy and reserved, I know you're gonna enjoy this recipe, too.

SLOPPY JOE BURGER

SERVINGS 4 **SERVING SIZE** 1 burger

- 1 lb regular or medium-ground beef
- ½ cup bell pepper, diced
- ½ cup onion, diced
- 2 cloves garlic, minced
- 2 tbsp chili powder
- 2 tsp paprika
- 1 tsp cumin
- 1 tsp thyme
- 1 tsp turmeric
- ½ tsp coriander
- 1 cup tomato sauce
- 2 tbsp powdered sweetener
- 2 tbsp coconut sauce
- 2 tbsp apple cider vinegar
- 1 tbsp Dijon mustard
- 2 tsp fish sauce
- ½ cup beef broth
- ½ tsp Xanthan gum (optional)
- Himalayan pink salt, and pepper, to taste

1. Sauté ground beef in a medium frying pan, crumbling and breaking it apart as it cooks.
2. Push meat back to the edges of the pan after 5 minutes, or after meat is mostly cooked.
3. Add pepper, onion, garlic, and spices directly to the oil in the pan and cook for 10 more minutes.
4. Add remaining ingredients and turn heat down to a simmer.
5. Continue to cook and allow the sauce to reduce to the point where there is no liquid at the bottom of the pan and the hamburger meat is coated in rich tomato flavour.
6. Serve on your favourite keto-friendly bun, or just spoon it up! You can also serve on a pizza, by itself on a plate, or in a lettuce cup.

note Macros are for sloppy joe mix only. Calculate your own macros for any bread used.

carbs	fibre	fat	protein
13g	3.5g	23g	24g

As a variation, dress this Sloppy Joe mix-up in style, and enjoy a Sloppy Joe Grilled Cheese! Add some of the Sloppy Joe mix to our grilled cheese recipe, found on page 96.

- 2 tbsp butter, melted
- 3 tbsp olive oil
- 4 large chicken breasts, boneless and skinless

FOR THE EGG WASH

- 2 eggs
- 3 tbsp water
- ¼ tsp pepper
- ¼ tsp salt

FOR THE FIRST DREDGE

- ½ cup coconut flour
- ½ tsp pepper
- ½ tsp salt

FOR THE SECOND DREDGE

- 1 cup almond flour
- 2 tsp Himalayan pink or sea salt
- 2 tsp garlic powder
- 1½ tsp onion powder
- 1 tsp chili powder
- 1 tsp dry mustard powder
- 1 tsp ground ginger
- 1 tsp ground thyme
- 1 tsp parsley
- 1 tsp dried oregano
- ½ tsp smoked paprika
- ½ tsp pepper
- ¼ tsp coriander
- ¼ tsp ground cumin

carbs	fibre	fat	protein
17g	9g	32g	42g

Our southern-fried oven chicken is a tweaked and revamped version of our Best-Ever Breaded Chicken recipe from our first book. This new oven version skips the pork rinds in the almond dredge, but adds another coconut dredge to the equation. The coconut flour dredge helps the egg stick to the chicken, and the egg wash in turn helps the final dredge hold, creating a final dish that is close to the chicken shack-style breaded chicken that you're used to. The butter/oil in the bottom of the pan adds a buttery note to the batter and takes this oven baked chicken up a notch in crunch.

I know the amount of ingredients and number of steps can look intimidating here. If you buy the spices/flours in bulk (think future batches!) and just take your time with the steps, you'll find it's super easy once you get the process down.

note **When we do the flip midway through, we spray dry battered areas with a coating of oil to ensure the entire piece of chicken will achieve that southern fried crispy texture.**

SOUTHERN FRIED OVEN CHICKEN

SERVINGS 4 **SERVING SIZE** 1 chicken breast

1. Heat the oven to 375°F.
2. Place melted butter and oil in the bottom of a baking dish. We use a foil-lined sheet tray.
3. Combine the eggs, water, and seasonings in a bowl big enough to hold these ingredients and also a chicken breast. Give yourself some space in the bowl to work and move the meat around. Set aside.

We use three utensils here: a fork for the wet mixture, and then fork-spoon combos for the two flour dredges–the forks for lifting and shaking excess coating, and the spoons to ensure a complete coating.

For fast cooking, flatten the chicken breasts slightly to an even thickness, or use cutlets. Place them between two pieces of plastic wrap and use a rolling pin or the bottom of a pot to flatten. They will cook quicker if you make them thinner, so be careful not to overcook. Turn them at about 10 minutes and check for doneness after another 5 minutes.

4. Combine the coconut-flour dredge and set aside.
5. Mix all the almond flour items together with a whisk and set aside. You're now ready to proceed to coating the chicken.
6. Arrange your components in the following order on your work space for ease of assembly:
    1. coconut flour dredge
    2. egg wash
    3. almond coating dredge
    4. prepared baking tray
7. Gently place your first chicken pieces into the coconut-flour dredge, and make sure to press the flour into the chicken. We use a fork to move the chicken in and then a spoon to move the flour to properly coat the meat.
8. Using a second dry fork, lift the chicken out of the coconut flour, shaking gently to remove extra dredge before dipping into the egg mixture.

9. Coat your chicken with the egg wash, taking care not to rub off the coconut layer. After coating the chicken in egg, move to the final almond-flour dredge.
10. Using your spoon-fork combo, completely cover your chicken in dredge. Remember to press the mixture into the chicken or it won't stick.
11. Give your chicken a gentle shake to remove excess coating before removing your chicken from the almond dredge.
12. Place your now-battered chicken on your prepared pan.
13. Repeat steps for remaining chicken pieces, then place pan in oven and bake 20 minutes.
14. Remove from the oven, carefully flip chicken pieces (we use a spatula) and cook for an additional 10-15 minutes.

As a variation, try this recipe as chicken nuggets or fingers. Same process, same ingredients, just cut your chicken into the desired size, slightly reduce cook time (use your meat thermometer), and follow the recipe as is!

Sometimes you just need to get good and sticky when you dig into a scrumptious dish. This recipe definitely fits that bill! The bourbon gives it a sinfully decadent kick, while the added sweetener mimics honey to give you the perfect sticky piece of chicken.

You can use any portion of the chicken for this recipe, but our very favourite is the thighs. They're higher in fat content and much more flavourful than the breast. This recipe, with crispy, skin-on thighs is such a delightful thing!

note **Make the sauce ahead of time and add it to your choice of chicken cut.**

STICKY KENTUCKY BOURBON CHICKEN

SERVINGS 6 **SERVING SIZE** 2 chicken thighs

- 2 tbsp olive oil
- ½ medium onion, chopped
- 2 cloves garlic, minced
- 1 tsp ginger, grated
- 2 cups tomato sauce
- 1½ cups powdered sweetener
- ⅔ cup bourbon
- ⅓ cup coconut sauce
- ¼ cup apple cider vinegar
- 1 tsp Korean chili flakes
- 1 tsp Himalayan pink or sea salt
- 1 tsp paprika
- 1 tsp oregano
- 1 tsp parsley
- ¼ tsp pepper
- pinch nutmeg
- 12 chicken thighs—we prefer chicken thighs, but you can use any cut

FOR THE SAUCE

1. Add oil and onions to saucepan and sauté for 3-5 minutes over medium heat. I often add about ¼ cup of water here to help the onions get soft.
2. Add garlic and ginger; continue to cook for 2-3 minutes. Adjust liquid if the pan starts to dry out.
3. Add remaining ingredients and simmer for 10 minutes.
4. Set aside to cool. Blend in a bullet or blender if you want a smooth sauce.

FOR THE CHICKEN

1. Preheat oven to 300°F.
2. Arrange chicken pieces in a baking dish and cover with sticky Kentucky sauce.
3. Bake covered in the preheated oven until thighs are cooked through and sauce is bubbling, about 50-55 minutes, or until internal temperature of chicken reaches 165°F. Check occasionally to spoon sauce over the thighs.
4. Remove chicken from the oven and uncover.
5. Turn oven to 400°F broil setting.

note **For calculating nutrition, one serving is 2 chicken thighs. If using chicken breasts, reduce portions by half, for 1 piece per serving.**

carbs	fibre	fat	protein
9.7g	1.5g	20g	20g

6. Spoon sauce over the thighs and return to the oven with the door slightly ajar.

   note Keep an eye at this stage so the sauce doesn't burn while caramelizing on the thighs.

7. Remove when the sauce on the chicken skin is bubbling slightly and turning brown.

   note I remove the chicken from the oven once and add more sauce, to make them extra saucy.

Serve alongside shirataki rice, with a side salad, or with a serving of keto-friendly fries.

These sweet and sour meatballs make the most delicious appetizers you've ever tasted! All you need is a toothpick and you're good to go. Add some cubed veggies to turn this into a full meal.

SWEET 'N' SOUR MEATBALLS

SERVINGS 8 **SERVING SIZE** 4 meatballs

FOR THE MEATBALLS

- 2 lb ground meat, can be chicken or beef
- 1 lb ground pork
- ⅓ cup pork rinds, crushed
- ¼ cup Parmesan cheese, grated
- 1 large egg
- 1 medium onion, finely chopped
- 3 large cloves garlic, minced
- 1 tsp paprika
- 1 parsley
- 1 tsp oregano
- 1 tsp Himalayan pink salt
- 1 tsp fennel seeds
- ½ tsp thyme
- ¼ tsp pepper

FOR THE SAUCE

- ¾ cup vinegar
- ¾ cup powdered sweetener
- ¾ cup tomato sauce
- ½ cup water
- ¼ cup coconut sauce
- 1 tsp garlic powder
- 1 tsp thyme
- 1 tsp turmeric
- 1 tsp Korean chili flakes
- 1 tsp salt
- ¼ tsp Xanthan gum, to sprinkle
- 1 cup bell peppers, cut into 1-inch squares (optional)
- 1 cup mushrooms, roughly chopped (optional)

1. Combine all meatball ingredients with a very light hand.

   note **The more you handle the mixture, the tougher the meatballs will be.**

2. Carefully form the meat into 32 balls about 1 inches in diameter.
3. Sauté meatballs in a large frying pan over medium heat until cooked through, turning them often to make sure they cook on all sides.
4. Remove meatballs from the frying pan and place them in an oven-safe casserole dish. Set aside.
5. Combine all sauce ingredients except Xanthan gum into a saucepan over medium heat, and whisk.
6. Cook for about 10 minutes and then remove from heat.
7. Sprinkle Xanthan gum over the sauce slowly and whisk to combine, then pour over the precooked meatballs. If using, add bell peppers and mushrooms when the dish is going in the oven.
8. Bake for 30-45 minutes.
9. Serve.

carbs	fibre	fat	protein
5.75g	1.1g	38g	38g

- 2 tsp oregano
- 2 tsp thyme
- 2 tsp garlic
- 1 tsp paprika
- 1 tsp basil
- 1 tsp onion powder
- ½ tsp Himalayan pink salt
- ½ tsp coriander
- ½ tsp pepper
- ½ can (28 oz can) San Marzano tomatoes, chopped
- 1 cup tomato sauce
- 4 veal chops, baked as described in Southern Fried Oven Chicken (see recipe page 152)
- 1 cup mozzarella, shredded
- ½ cup Parmesan, shredded

In this dish, we cook the breaded meat ahead of time then snuggle it into our rustic marinara sauce and cheese, to get twice the flavour. If you have guests coming and you want a worry-free event, you can make the battered veal as well as the sauce ahead of time. Then, put it all together at the last minute.

note **Chicken, pork, or any other meat can be swapped in to replace the veal, if desired.**

VEAL PARMESAN

SERVINGS 4 **SERVING SIZE** 1 veal chop

1. Combine spices, chopped tomatoes, and sauce in a medium-size bowl, then spoon into the bottom of a baking dish. Lay the baked veal right into the sauce and place in a 325°F oven for 15 minutes.
2. Remove baking dish from the oven and cover veal with mozzarella, then top with Parmesan.
3. Return to the oven for 10 more minutes or until the cheese has thoroughly melted and is just starting to turn golden brown on top.

carbs	fibre	fat	protein
11.5g	2.75g	20g	35g

Serve with a green or Caesar salad.

The idea for this recipe came to us as we watched an international cooking show, where a dish was cooked and then finished by pouring vinegar over over the battered chops in the pan. I couldn't get my head around how this dish would taste or how it would turn out. We just love watching food and cooking shows; you can almost taste the flawlessly presented dishes that show up on your TV screen, but this one eluded me—until I decided to make it my own.

We tweaked and taste-tested and came up with our own version of this recipe, and we just love it. It's reminiscent of a sweet and sour dish, but much simpler and in some ways more refined and to the point. Try it for yourself!

VINEGAR PORK CHOPS

SERVINGS 2 **SERVING SIZE** 1 battered pork chop

2 pieces boneless pork chop, 6-8 oz each

FOR THE EGG WASH

1 egg

½ cup water

½ tsp salt

¼ tsp pepper

FOR THE DREDGE

2 cups pork rinds, crushed

1 tsp garlic powder

1 tsp Himalayan pink salt

½ tsp fresh-cracked pepper

keto-friendly oil such as lard, olive oil, coconut oil, for frying

½ cup vinegar

1. Pound the pork pieces flat with a tenderizing mallet or a rolling pin, and pat them dry with a paper towel. *note* **We cover our meat top and bottom with plastic wrap first, to reduce raw meat splatter.**
2. Combine egg, water, and seasonings for the wash. Whisk to fully incorporate.
3. Soak the pork pieces in the egg wash while you work on the dredge.
4. Crush the pork rinds using a rolling pin or mallet, or grind them up in a bullet. Add seasonings to the pork rinds and stir to combine.
5. Place the dredge in a shallow dish, like a pie plate. Using a fork, remove the pork pieces from the egg wash one at a time. Place the individual pieces into the dredge and press the mixture into the meat.
6. Fry the pork over medium heat in a deep-sided sauté pan for a shallow fry, or in a deep fryer for about 5 minutes per side or until the pork reaches an internal temperature of 145°F.
7. Remove from pan and turn off the burner/deep-fryer.
8. Carefully drain most of the hot oil from the pan, and discard later. Return the pan to medium heat.
9. When the pan is hot again, place the chops in the pan and pour vinegar directly over the chops. Let the pork sizzle for 30 seconds, then flip them over for another 30 seconds, so that both sides get coated.
10. Serve immediately.

carbs	fibre	fat	protein
2g	0g	52g	38g

Is Portion Control Necessary

Let's talk portions for carb replacements and how to compose your plate. The main part of your ketogenic diet should be filled with real unprocessed meat/fish and green leafy veggies.

Our habits from the past often have us eating a huge portion of carb replacements in a big pile in the middle of the plate, with a side of veggies and meat. This can get you into keto trouble, very fast. We need a smaller portion size for these items.

Carb replacements should only be occasional items at best, not every day, and certainly not every meal. If you choose to have them on your plate, it should make up no more than ⅓ of your plate.

What do we mean by carb replacements? They include cauliflower faux-tatoes, cauliflower mac and cheese, daikon or celeriac (celery root) dishes, pasta replacements, konjac rice, and almond/coconut flour dishes.

While these are keto-friendly, they are still higher in carbs and should be eaten in moderation.

SIDES

Chinese-Style Faux Fried Rice | 164

Chioggia Beet Salad | 167

Daikon Asian Slaw | 168

Garlic Butter Noodles | 171

Pike House Italian Salad | 172

PEI Faux-tato Pie | 174

Scalloped Spaghetti Squash | 177

Spanish Rice | 178

Thai Red Curry Noodles | 181

Twice-Baked and Loaded Cauliflower | 182

Warm German Faux-Tato Salad | 184

All macro counts given are per serving.

Mom had the best egg-fried rice. I remember as a child whenever we ate out at a Chinese restaurant as a family, I always felt disappointed with the rice they would serve. It just never stacked up to Mom's. I honestly think Mom's cooking spoiled me for life.

Real rice wouldn't be keto-friendly, as it is full of starch and would cause a blood glucose spike, but konjac rice is good to go. Just be careful not to overload your plate with these replacement items; even though they're keto-friendly, they are a little carb-y.

One taste of this rice brought me right back to Mom's kitchen. Hoping it brings you to a happy place as well.

CHINESE-STYLE FAUX FRIED RICE

SERVINGS 6 **SERVING SIZE** ⅓ cup

- 1 tbsp keto-friendly fat, such as bacon fat, butter
- ½ medium onion, diced
- ½ cup pork, chicken, or beef, diced
- ½ cup peppers, diced
- 2 cloves garlic, minced
- 1 tsp turmeric
- 1 tsp ginger powder
- ½ tsp garam masala
- ½ tsp coriander
- ½ tsp Himalayan pink salt
- 2 eggs, whisked
- ⅓ cup coconut sauce
- 1 pack of konjac rice or 2 cups of precooked cauliflower rice
- ¼ cup fresh cilantro or parsley, chopped

1. Sauté onion in fat until translucent.
2. Add meat, peppers and garlic and continue to cook for 5 more minutes.
3. Add spices and stir to incorporate.
4. Break the eggs right into the pan and stir the pan contents into the egg, making sure that egg is coating the meat and veggies as it cooks.
5. Add coconut sauce and rice, and continue to cook over medium-low until the sauce has fully reduced and the rice has warmed throughout.
5. Garnish with cilantro or parsley and serve.

carbs	fibre	fat	protein
6.5g	1.5g	4g	6g

Don't overeat carb replacements. These items should make up ⅓ of your plate at most!

Beets are one of those veggies that us ketonians eat very sparingly, as they are a root veggie and slightly higher in carbs that those that grow above the earth. This raw beet salad uses the Chioggia or candy cane beet. With only 9.56 carbs and 2.8 fibre per 100g, they aren't so bad after all. These and other root veggies should be avoided in the early days of keto; at this point, you're trying to teach your body to forget about sugar, so the natural sugars in the beets would not be helpful, but they are fine in moderation after you're fat-adapted.

Chioggia or candy cane beets are an Italian heirloom variety native to Chioggia, Italy, and were first discovered in 1840. The colourful veggies will create a delicious earthy flavour and also a vibrant and vivid show on your plates—one that your guests will not soon forget, in a very good way!

CHIOGGIA BEET SALAD

SERVINGS 4 **SERVING SIZE** ¼ of the salad

- 1 candy cane beet, sliced thinly
- ¼ cup white balsamic vinegar
- 2 cups spinach or spring greens
- 6 basil leaves, chopped
- ⅛ cup pecans, chopped
- ⅛ cup goat cheese, crumbled
- ⅓ cup extra-virgin olive oil
- 1 tsp Dijon mustard
- ¼ tsp dried basil
- Himalayan pink salt, and pepper, to taste

1. Slice the beet super thin with a mandolin.

   note **Use a mandolin with a guard to get those beets sliced super thin. Careful of your fingers!**

2. Soak the raw beet in white balsamic vinegar for 15 minutes.
3. Remove beets from the vinegar and reserve ⅛ cup of the liquid for the dressing.
4. Add the spinach as the base of the salad in a bowl.
5. Next, layer the beet over the spinach leaves.
6. Sprinkle the chopped basil, pecans, and cheese on top of the beet.
7. Combine the reserved vinegar, olive oil, mustard, basil, and salt and pepper, and whisk or shake to emulsify. We use a tiny whisk. Pour dressing over salad and serve.

Don't throw out the excess vinegar after soaking the beet. It's full of flavour and can add a pop of colour to any dish!

carbs	fibre	fat	protein
5.5g	1.25g	28g	2.5g

If you like Asian food flavours, or are fan of kimchee, you're gonna love this daikon Asian slaw. It has crunch, heat, and oodles of flavour. Stack the serving on the plate for an eye-pleasing presentation!

Daikon Asian Slaw pairs particularly well with pork, but you can use this slaw as a side for any dish! Try it atop a pulled pork sandwich or burger! You'll be amazed at how much it amps up the flavour. This salad is best served as soon as it's made, but can be held in the fridge for a day or so.

DAIKON ASIAN SLAW

SERVINGS 6 **SERVING SIZE** ⅓ cup of slaw

- 2 cups daikon radish, peeled and julienned
- 1 carrot, ribboned or grated
- ¼ red onion, sliced thin
- ¼ cup extra virgin olive oil or light sesame seed oil, cold or expeller pressed, not toasted
- 3 tbsp white or apple cider vinegar
- 2 tbsp powdered sweetener
- 1 tbsp coconut sauce
- 1 tbsp lime juice
- 1½ tsp Korean chili flakes
- 1 tsp chili paste or hot sauce, to taste
- 1 tsp fish sauce
- ¼ cup green onions or chives, diced, for garnish

1. Mix all ingredients in a medium-size mixing bowl, and serve immediately.

carbs	fibre	fat	protein
6.7g	1.7g	10g	1g

Garlic Butter Noodles are packed with flavour and will serve as the perfect accompaniment to any meat dish. This isn't a thick sauce that will coat your noodles like a tomato or alfredo sauce; instead, it's a light and aromatic blend of broth and oils that perfectly balance and delight the palate.

Try it once and you'll be a true fan.

GARLIC BUTTER NOODLES

SERVINGS 4 **SERVING SIZE** ¼ of the recipe

- 6 tbsp butter
- 8 cloves garlic, minced
- 2 tsp thyme
- 1 tsp basil
- 1 tsp thyme
- 1 tsp Korean chili flakes
- 1 tsp salt
- 1 tsp black pepper
- 1 cup chicken or veggie broth
- 1 large bunch baby spinach, chopped—we use about 2 cups
- 6-8 baby tomatoes, diced
- Parmesan cheese, shredded
- 1 package konjac noodles or spiralized zoodles—we use angel hair Nupasta

1. Heat the butter and garlic in a large non-stick sauté pan over low heat for 2-3 minutes, taking care not to burn the garlic.
2. Add spices to the pan and then the broth, and simmer for 5-10 minutes.
3. Add spinach and tomatoes to the pan and stir to incorporate. Continue to cook until the spinach and tomato have wilted.
4. Stir in Parmesan cheese. Simmer for 5 minutes to reduce to your desired consistency.

   note **We like ours more like a wet noodle with a little sauce; you might enjoy yours a little saucier.**

5. Stir in the pasta and allow it 2-3 minutes to heat. Serve.

carbs	fibre	fat	protein
7.75g	4g	19g	4g

Salad dressings are hard when you first start keto! If you're clean keto, you're quick to find that most commercial recipes are not suitable; they're either full of chemicals or loaded with inflammatory veggie oils. This is the salad dressing you will find most often in our fridge! We make it in small batches in a Mason jar and use often.

Our house dressing salad is a light and easy Italian salad blend that works well as a stand-alone meal, a starter, or a side salad. The dressing can even double as a meat marinade!

PIKE HOUSE ITALIAN SALAD

SERVINGS 4 **SERVING SIZE** ¼ of the salad and dressing

FOR THE DRESSING

- ¼ cup keto-friendly oil—we used olive oil
- 2 tbsp apple cider vinegar
- 2 tbsp Parmesan cheese, grated
- 1 tbsp Dijon mustard
- 1 tbsp keto mayo (see recipe on page 227 in our first book)
- 1 tbsp lemon juice
- 1 tsp garlic powder
- 1 tsp oregano
- ½ tsp onion powder or dehydrated flakes
- ½ tsp basil
- ½ tsp red pepper flakes
- ¼ tsp rosemary
- ¼ tsp tarragon

FOR THE SALAD

- 2 cups iceberg lettuce, shredded
- ¼ red onion, thinly sliced
- 4 small pickled peppers, whole
- 2 small vine-ripened tomato, cut into wedges
- ½ cup pork rinds, chopped into croutons
- 1 tbsp Parmesan cheese, grated
- ½ tsp Himalayan pink salt
- freshly cracked pepper, to taste
- 2 tbsp sliced black olives (optional)

1. Add all dressing ingredients to a blender, or shake it up in a Mason jar like we do.
2. Assemble salad in a large bowl and use the red onion, peppers, tomato, olives, croutons (pork rinds), and cheese as garnish.
3. Toss the salad at tableside.

carbs	fibre	fat	protein
6g	2g	20g	6g

NOT A FAN OF ITALIAN DRESSING?

Try these alternate dressings!

MUSTARD VINAIGRETTE

A fresh and vibrant dressing for a green salad.

- ¾ cup olive oil
- ⅔ cup green onions, minced
- ¼ cup Dijon mustard
- 3 tbsp white wine vinegar
- 1 tbsp powdered sweetener
- 2 tsp sage or tarragon
- 1 clove garlic, minced, or 1 tsp garlic powder
- 1 tsp rosemary
- Himalayan pink salt, and pepper, to taste

1. Combine all ingredients and drizzle over your favourite green salad. For added zip add a couple of dashes of your favourite hot sauce.

servings 12 x ⅛ cup **carbs** 0.5g **fibre** 0.25g **fat** 14g **protein** 0g

ONION-POPPY SEED SALAD DRESSING

This onion-poppy seed dressing is simply gorgeous on a green salad. Our very favourite is a base of green leafies, chopped strawberries, pecans, and crumbled goat cheese with a generous portion of this dressing.

- ⅓ cup powdered sweetener
- ½ cup white vinegar
- 1 tsp Himalayan pink salt
- 1 tsp dry mustard
- 1 tsp onion, minced
- ½ cup olive oil
- ½ cup avocado oil
- 1 tbsp poppy seeds

1. Place all ingredients in a Mason jar and shake vigorously to combine. Enjoy on your favourite green salad.

servings 8 x ⅛ cup **carbs** 0g **fibre** 0g **fat** 28g **protein** 0g

RANCH DRESSING, ECK STYLE

This ranch is a variation of our Caesar dressing, dressed up with a different flavour profile. Most ranch dressings have a creamy dairy base, while Caesar is more of a fancy emulsified vinaigrette. We love taking the same old unhealthy recipes and turning them on their head. I know, this one isn't the same. You just gotta keep in mind that 'the same' is what got us unhealthy in the first place, isn't it? Try our recipe, we know you're gonna be a believer.

- ¾ cup olive oil
- ¼ cup avocado oil
- ¼ cup coconut oil
- ½ cup Parmesan cheese, grated
- 1 tbsp Dijon mustard
- 3 tbsp apple cider vinegar
- 1 tsp garlic powder
- 1 tsp onion powder
- 1 tsp dried minced onion flakes
- 2 tsp dried parsley
- 1 tsp dried dill weed
- 1 tsp salt
- ½ tsp black pepper
- 1 tsp powdered sweetener
- Himalayan pink salt, and pepper, to taste
- 3 tbsp lemon juice
- 1 egg, room temperature

1. Blend all ingredients except egg in an immersion blender or bullet.
2. Add egg to the mix and allow it to sink to the bottom
3. Place blender on the bottom and slowly blend; move the blender slowly through the mixture as it thickens.
4. Use right away, or refrigerate for up to a week.

servings 16 x ⅛ cup **carbs** 0.75g **fibre** 0g **fat** 18g **protein** 1g

This dish has its origins in French cooking. *Pommes Anna*, or Anna potatoes, is a classic dish of sliced, layered potatoes cooked in a large amount of melted butter. We started playing with this concept early in our keto days, and in our first book we zigzagged into a dauphinoise. This resulted in our scalloped daikon dish that you all know and love.

Once the first book was done and dusted, our quest to perfect potatoes Anna got our attention once again. Like any good ketonian, we turned to the bacon wrap. Our bacon-wrapped faux-tato pie was a thing of wonder right from the get-go, and only needed a few tweaks to elevate it to ECK level. It was oh so good!

We tested our recipe with family, and quickly learned that there was a dish similar to our ketofied faux-tato Anna that was quite popular in PEI. So, in honour of the kind folks from Prince Edward Island, we changed the outside bacon wrap, and also changed the recipe name to PEI Faux-tato Pie. We hope you love it!

PEI FAUX-TATO PIE

SERVINGS 8 **SERVING SIZE** ⅛ of the pie

- 1 tsp salt
- 1 large daikon radish, thinly sliced
- 1 package bacon
- 1 onion, thinly sliced
- 1 tsp garlic powder
- ½ tsp pepper
- 2 cups old cheddar, shredded
- 1 cup Parmesan cheese, shredded

carbs	fibre	fat	protein
3g	1.2g	27g	17g

1. Add salt to large pot of water and bring to a boil.
2. Parboil the daikon slices for 20 minutes, then set aside to cool. The slices should be starting to soften, but not be mushy.
3. Preheat your oven to 350°F.
4. Line the bottom of a pie plate with a round sheet of parchment paper.
6. Start arranging your bacon slices on the bottom of your pie plate. Imagine a clock; place your first slice at the centre of the plate, and extend the strip to the 12 o'clock position. Half of the bacon slice should be in a line coming from the centre of the plate, with the other half hanging down over the edge.
7. Next place the 6, then the 3 and the 9, taking care to only slightly overlap each edge in the centre. You want them touching, but not in a big heap.
8. Continue laying pieces around the clock, with every layer moving the slices of bacon back a bit towards the edge of the pan so they're not overlapping too much in the centre.

note **When you're done most of the edge of the pie plate will be covered with bacon, with pie base totally covered in bacon.**

You can use more bacon to fully enclose the edges if you prefer full coverage, but be aware this adds extra fat that will have to be drained from your dish.

9. Place the sliced onion together with 3 tbsp water in a microwave-safe dish and cook for 2 minutes, until the onions are translucent and partially cooked.
10. Cover the bottom of the pie with ⅓ of the Parmesan cheese.
11. Begin laying the radish slices in the bottom of the pan, overlapping them so the entire bottom is now covered with sliced daikon.
12. Place about ¼ of the onion on top of the radish and then add a sprinkle of pepper and about ⅓ of the cheddar.
13. Continue with another layer of radish, then ⅓ the grated Parmesan, using a sprinkle of garlic powder this time.
14. Continue layering, alternating between the two cheeses until your dish is stacked high in the middle, with the edges being about the height of the rim of your pan.
15. Begin to bring your pieces of bacon up over the top of your pan. Start with the last pieces of bacon you added and work your way backwards, so that last in is first out. Start at the corner of the clock; 2, 7, 5, 8, etc., finishing with the first pieces you added at 3, 9, 6 and 12.

Make sure to cover the pie top and bottom with parchment.

note **Your faux-tato pie should now be totally covered with bacon.**

16. Use a round of parchment to cover the bacon, and then place a heavy cover on top of the parchment to hold everything in place until the daikon is fully cooked and the bacon has set.
17. Place the completed pie on a sheet tray with an edged lip to catch any spilled bacon fat.
18. Bake your pie for at least 1 hour. Time will vary depending on your oven and the thickness of your pie.
19. Remove the pie from the oven and carefully take off the cover and parchment to check for doneness. The daikon will be soft when pierced with a knife, if it is fully cooked.
20. Carefully drain excess fat, or use rolled-up pieces of paper towel as a sponge to sop up excess bacon fat.
21. Return your pie to the oven uncovered, to crisp the bacon. This part takes time, and all ovens will differ, so keep checking your pie every 5 minutes. Rotate the dish in the oven each time. All bacon should be crispy on top.
22. Let the pie rest for at least 10 minutes, and then cover with a plate and flip out onto a serving plate. Slice and enjoy!

We freeze our leftover slices individually on a sheet tray, then place the frozen pieces in a freezer bag for individual servings. Leftovers freeze well for an easy and quick take-out side dish in the future.

Lots of people love spaghetti squash but are unsure what to do with it. We often have it on the side with just a little butter, salt, and pepper, but this scalloped dish is our all-time favourite!

Scalloped squash is great as a side dish, or you can add a thinly sliced chicken breast or two and some extra veggies to make this a delicious crowd-pleasing, stand-alone casserole.

SCALLOPED SPAGHETTI SQUASH

SERVINGS 8 **SERVING SIZE** ½ cup

- 1 medium-large spaghetti squash, about 4 cups
- 2 tbsp butter
- 1 cup onion, sliced
- 1 cup cheddar cheese, grated
- ½ cup sour cream—beware of starches here
- ½ cup cream cheese, room temperature
- ⅛ cup coconut flour
- 1 tbsp Dijon mustard
- 1 tsp parsley
- 1 tsp thyme
- 1 tsp garlic powder
- ½ tsp onion powder
- ½ tsp ancho chili
- ½ tsp pepper
- 1 cup old cheddar, for garnish
- 1 tsp paprika, for garnish

1. Cut the spaghetti squash in half and remove the seeds. You can either pre-bake for 45-60 minutes (depending on size) in the oven or place in a covered dish with the bottom covered with water, and microwave for 10-12 minutes. Set aside to cool.
2. Add butter to a medium-size sauté pan over medium heat. Sauté onion for 5 minutes or until onions are translucent.
3. Add the remaining ingredients and reduce heat to a simmer at low-medium for about 10 minutes. Set aside to cool.
4. Using a fork, scrape the insides of the squash and transfer into the cheese sauce; mix to combine.
5. Transfer to a casserole dish and bake at 375°F for 1 hour.
6. Remove from oven and sprinkle the garnish items over the casserole.
7. Return to oven and bake for another 10 minutes, or until cheese is melted.

Jazz up this recipe up by mixing in thinly sliced precooked chicken breast, rustic cut mushrooms, or bell peppers–or some of each!

carbs	fibre	fat	protein
10.6g	2.25g	18g	8g

The pre-keto version of this dish came from a commercially available package where we just added a little salsa to fancy it up. When we started our journey of health, we knew we could do better. As we were stepping away from processed foods, we just used regular rice and our own spice mix, but as we began our low-carb and then keto lifestyle, we took this dish to the final recipe you see here today. Fully keto!

This totally amped up and ketofied recipe calls for konjac or cauliflower rice. We like this dish a little on the moist and sticky side; cook it longer if you like your rice to have a drier consistency

SPANISH RICE

SERVINGS 4 **SERVING SIZE** ¼ of recipe

- 1 tbsp keto-friendly fat, such as bacon fat, butter
- ½ medium onion, diced
- 1 package of konjac rice or 2 cups of precooked cauliflower rice.
- 2 cloves garlic, minced
- 1 tbsp chili powder
- 2 tsp cumin powder
- ½ tsp Himalayan pink salt
- 1 tbsp coconut sauce
- ¼ cup black olives, chopped
- ¾ cup of salsa
- ¼ cup of fresh cilantro or parsley, chopped

1. Sauté onion in fat until translucent, and set aside.
2. Drain, rinse, and dry fry rice and garlic until the original packaging liquid and water has completely cooked off and the garlic is cooked.
3. Mix in spices, coconut sauce, olives, and salsa and continue to fry for around 5 minutes.
4. Add onion back to the pan and stir to incorporate.
5. Just before serving, stir in the cilantro or parsley.

carbs	fibre	fat	protein
8.75g	4g	6g	1.25g

Optionally, top with a dollop of clean sour cream and extra salsa.

This medium-heat dish is full of flavour but it's not overly spicy. Increase the spices to suit your own tastes if you like it spicier.

THAI RED CURRY NOODLES

SERVINGS 4 **SERVING SIZE** ¼ of the noodles

- 2 tbsp oil
- ½ medium onion, diced
- ½ cup peppers, diced
- 1 cup spinach, packed
- 2 cloves garlic, minced
- 2 tbsp coconut sauce
- 1 tsp red curry paste
- 1 tsp curry
- 1 tsp turmeric
- ½ tsp cardamom
- ½ tsp Korean chili flakes
- ¼ tsp garam masala
- 1 cup chicken or veggie broth
- salt and pepper to taste—we used 1 tsp salt and ½ tsp pepper
- 1 pack konjac noodles or 2 cups cauliflower rice or spiralized zoodles

1. Add oil to a medium-size sauté pan over medium heat.
2. Add onions and sauté for 5 minutes or until onions become translucent.
3. Add peppers, spinach, and garlic. Continue to cook until spinach is wilted, about 5 minutes.
4. Add coconut sauce, curry paste, spices, and broth and continue to cook for about 10 minutes.
5. Add konjac noodles/cauliflower rice/zoodles and turn heat down to a simmer.
6. Cook until noodles are heated throughout.

carbs	fibre	fat	protein
8g	3g	8g	1g

This recipe took a lot of trial and error on our part. Our first versions included frozen cauliflower (too soggy), not enough whipping cream and sour cream (too dry, not creamy enough), and no spices (not enough flavour). It was starting to sound like the culinary version of Goldilocks and the Three Bears! We just couldn't get it right.

I'm not a fan of cauliflower disguised as anything other than what it is—a cauliflower—but for some reason, this recipe works for our taste buds. For us, it took the extra steps of making sure all the water was pressed out, and then blending it up until it was super smooth. We didn't like the mouth feel of those tiny florets in the mix; it didn't feel like mashed potatoes, it just wasn't right. They screamed counterfeit and wasn't the ketofied 'potato' fix we were looking for.

This twice-baked and loaded cauliflower casserole tastes just like loaded baked potato, without the loaded carbs and calories. This side dish pairs well with a grilled steak, or any other meat dish you would serve alongside mashed potatoes.

TWICE-BAKED AND LOADED CAULIFLOWER

SERVINGS 8 **SERVING SIZE** ¼ cup

- 1 large head cauliflower
- 4 oz cream cheese
- ¼ cup 35% whipping cream
- 6 slices bacon, cooked and crumbled
- ½ cup sour cream
- ¼ tsp cumin
- ¼ tsp coriander
- ¼ tsp garlic powder
- ¼ cup green onions, minced
- ¼ cup Parmesan cheese, grated
- 1 cup old cheddar cheese, shredded

note Check the ingredients in your sour cream; many of these are full of starches!

1. Preheat oven to 350°F. Cut out stem/core from cauliflower and cut cauliflower into small pieces. This is still food, so don't throw it away.
2. Boil cauliflower in a large pot of salted water until tender.
3. Drain well in a colander and then press between sheets of paper towels to get out as much water as possible.
4. Transfer cauliflower to a mixing bowl and mash with potato masher.

   note We like ours super smooth, like creamy mashed potatoes, so we usually take the extra step of blending it in a bullet until all florets have disappeared.

carbs	fibre	fat	protein
3.75g	1.5g	13.5g	6g

Wringing the cauliflower in a kitchen towel is another way to ensure you've moved most of the water.

5. Mix in cream cheese, whipping cream, and ¾ of the crumbled bacon.
6. Spread evenly in a medium-size greased casserole dish. Bake covered in a 350°F oven for 15 minutes.
7. Remove from the oven, and mix in the sour cream, spices, green onion, and Parmesan cheese.
8. Sprinkle the top with cheddar cheese, and reserved bacon.
9. Bake uncovered, 10-15 minutes more, or until hot and bubbly.

The original recipe was a family favourite that we learned years ago from friends who were of German descent. It was my first exposure to a warm potato salad and let me tell ya, I was so impressed! I like regular potato salads, but this new warm version took dinner to a whole new level.

Make sure to only use small portions of this salad. While it's keto-friendly, any starch replacement would still be carb-y. A full 'cold plate' with two or three faux-tato salads would not be your friend if keto is your life choice—way too many carbs at one sitting. Opt for one type of faux-tato salad, with just one small serving. Easy does it. While this salad is lovely cold, it really does best warm, alongside some meat and veggies fresh off the grill.

WARM GERMAN FAUX-TATO SALAD

SERVINGS 8 **SERVING SIZE** ⅛ of the recipe

- 1 large celeriac/celery root, approximately 1 lb peeled, and cut into 1-inch cubes
- ½ cup 35% whipping cream
- 1½ cups water
- 1 tsp Himalayan pink salt
- ¼ tsp freshly ground pepper

FOR THE DRESSING

- ½ cup mayo (see recipe on page 227 in our first book)
- 4 strips bacon, diced
- ½ cup apple cider vinegar
- 2 tbsp avocado or olive oil
- 1 tbsp chives, minced
- 1 tbsp Dijon mustard
- 2 tsp powdered sweetener, to taste
- 2 tsp garlic powder
- 1 tsp onion powder
- 1 tsp Himalayan pink salt
- ½ tsp pepper
- 1 tbsp chopped chives, to garnish

carbs	fibre	fat	protein
6.5g	1.25g	20g	3g

FOR THE SALAD

1. Peel celeriac, making certain to carefully dig out any cracks and crevices that could have soil or dirt.
2. Bring whipping cream, water, and salt to a boil in a large saucepan over medium-high heat.
3. Add celeriac cubes and garlic; bring to boil. Reduce heat to low-medium and simmer for 20 minutes, or until cubes are tender.
4. Drain and set aside.

FOR THE DRESSING

1. We recommend you mix this is in a separate bowl, so you can control how saucy your potato salad is. Because the salad isn't starchy, it will be different from a pre-keto potato salad. Add dressing a little at a time until you reach that sweet spot that's perfect for you.

Bacon can be reserved as garnish. We recommend eating this warm, but it's just as delightful when cold.

PUTTING IT TOGETHER

1. In a medium-size bowl while the celeriac is still warm, mash about half of your faux-tatoes. Using two knives, in the remaining bowl chop the faux-tatoes into smaller pieces.

   note **This is not meant to be a smooth-mashed salad; instead, it's meant to be textured, chopped, and rustic.**

2. Combine chopped and mashed celeriac, add dressing, and sprinkle the chopped chives as garnish.
3. Serve warm.

Little Things

When it comes to keto condiments it's all about keeping the portions small, so if you're a person who loved things coated in a thick layer of ketchup or BBQ sauce, we gently suggest you try to get used to a new normal. We have sweet sauces, savoury sauces, pickles and jellies, and a host of other tastes to add flavour to your life! Remember, these things are all extras, and are really just a tiny bit of tasty on the side.

SAUCES & EXTRAS

Embrace Your Saucy Side | 188

ECK #1 Keto Steak Sauce | 189

Big G Sauce | 190

Hoisin Sauce | 191

Fromage Burger Sauce | 192

Grandmudder's Green Chow | 195

Hot 'n' Bothered Rum Sauce | 196

Half-Sour Pickles | 198

Quickled Red Onion | 199

Sweet Adorable Mustard Pickles | 200

Dandelion Root Jelly | 203

Homemade Maraschino Cherries | 204

Islander Iced Cappuccino | 206

Paddy's Irish Shake | 207

Skinny Face Pizza Crust | 209

Smoked Salmon Dip | 210

Wraps, Wontons, and Fine Pastry | 213

All macro counts given are per serving.

EMBRACE YOUR SAUCY SIDE

**A little sauce can add a lot of flavour to a meal.
Try these sauce variations to really boost taste and change things up!**

SHED SAUCE

The origins of this sauce may have come from a restaurant chain, but you will find there aren't a lot of fancy chalets here in Newfoundland and Labrador. What we do have is sheds; lots and lots of backyard sheds! Serve this sauce with any protein, but it pairs especially well with chicken. You're gonna swear you're in the Swiss Alps, keto-style!

- 1 cup chicken broth
- ½ cup apple cider vinegar
- 2 tbsp tomato sauce
- 1 tsp salt
- 1 tsp powdered sweetener
- 1 tsp paprika
- 1 tsp garlic powder
- ½ tsp oregano
- ½ tsp onion powder
- ¼ tsp pepper
- ¼ tsp nutmeg
- ¼ tsp ground ginger
- ¼ tsp basil
- ¼ tsp Xanthan gum
- 1 tsp hot sauce (optional)

FIGHTING IRISH BBQ SAUCE

There's a strong Irish brogue found here in parts of Newfoundland; accents have been passed down through generations, after our ancestors came across the Pond from the motherland. The fiery personality often associated with the 'fighting Irish' comes to fruition here, as this sauce has some zing. We think you're gonna love it!

- 2 tbsp olive oil
- ½ onion, minced fine
- 2 tsp ginger, grated
- 2 cloves garlic, minced
- ¾ cup powdered sweetener
- 2 cups tomato sauce
- ¾ cup Irish whiskey
- ⅓ cup coconut sauce
- ⅓ cup white vinegar
- 2 tbsp hot sauce
- 1½ tsp Korean chili flakes
- 1 tsp paprika
- 1 tsp parsley
- 1 tsp Himalayan pink salt
- ½ tsp sage
- ½ tsp fennel seed, crushed
- ½ tsp cayenne
- ½ tsp pepper
- ¼ tsp nutmeg
- ⅛ tsp cinnamon

SCOTTISH HIGHLANDS GRILL SAUCE

A full-flavoured sticky and delicious BBQ sauce. You could add a little heather from the highlands for flavour, if you had it available to you. We chose a little thyme to boost the flavour here. The scotch adds a little extra something-something. Your friends are gonna love it, but won't quite be able to place the extra taste that comes from the Scottish whisky. Make sure you don't tell 'em our little secret.

- 2 tbsp olive oil
- ½ onion, minced fine
- 2 cloves garlic, minced
- ¾ cup powdered sweetener
- 2 cup tomato sauce
- ⅔ cup Scotch whisky
- ⅓ cup coconut sauce
- ⅓ cup apple cider vinegar
- 1 tsp Korean chili flakes
- 1 tsp ginger, grated
- 1 tsp Hungarian paprika or regular paprika
- 1 tsp thyme
- 1 tsp Himalayan pink salt
- ½ tsp pepper
- pinch nutmeg

TO MAKE THE SAUCE

note **First two steps are for Irish and Scottish sauces only, as there are no onions and garlic in Shed sauce.**

1. Add olive oil and onions to a saucepan and sauté for 3-5 minutes over medium heat. I often add about ¼ cup of water here to help coax the onions to get soft.
2. Add garlic and ginger; continue to cook for 2-3 minutes. Adjust liquid if the pan starts to dry out.
3. Add remaining ingredients and simmer for 10 minutes or until sauce reaches your desired consistency.
4. Sauces can be whizzed up in a blender if you prefer a smooth sauce.

We originally developed this recipe as a steak sauce for a keto version of steak and cheese pizza. A thin layer of this sauce is all you need to make your pizza go from good to downright amazing!

This sauce is a real show-stopper alongside a thick and juicy grilled steak, but also works well to have on the side of any meat that is looking for a little kick. Try it with grilled pork or chicken! It's not just for beef.

ECK #1 KETO STEAK SAUCE

SERVINGS 48 **SERVING SIZE** 1 teaspoon

1. Add all ingredients to a saucepan, whisk, and simmer for 15 minutes.
2. Cook and reduce until sauce reaches your desired consistency.
3. Let cool before use.
4. Blend with a stick blender or bullet for a smooth sauce.

- 1 clove garlic, minced
- ¼ cup water
- ¼ cup white vinegar
- ¼ cup tomato, roughly chopped
- ⅛ cup Dijon mustard
- 1 tbsp fish sauce
- 1 tbsp onion, minced
- ¼ tsp black pepper
- ¼ tsp celery seed
- ⅛ tsp Himalayan pink or sea salt
- pinch cayenne pepper
- zest of half an orange (optional)

carbs	fibre	fat	protein
0.4g	0g	0g	0g

Season your burgers with salt and pepper only; if you're adding binders and other fillers to the patty, you're making a mini meatloaf and not a burger. These extras are just going to mask what should be the star of your burger, the meat. The magic of the burger happens when you can taste the flavour of the meat as well as the sauces and toppings.

We held out a long time before trying our hand at this sauce. I've never been a big fan of the Big Mac; I always thought the sauce overwhelmed the flavour of what I like in a burger, the taste of the grilled meat. Maybe that was why Big Mac sauce wasn't on my radar early on.

Geoff was another story; he loved this burger and was known to scarf them down in multitudes in his pre-keto days. It was easy to tell we got this recipe spot on right out of the gate. He was almost drooling in anticipation when I dressed the plates after making this this first time. He near about floated to the ceiling like Snuffles, the cartoon dog, after just one bite. His feedback? "You knocked it outta the park, Missus." Needless to say, this one is named in tribute to the love of my life, my G.

BIG G SAUCE

SERVINGS 12 **SERVING SIZE** 1 tablespoon

- ½ cup keto mayo (see recipe on page 227 in our first book)
- 2 tbsp dill pickle, minced
- 2 tsp mustard
- 1 tsp dill pickle juice or white vinegar
- 1½ tbsp powdered sweetener
- 1 tsp garlic powder
- 1 tsp onion powder
- 1 tsp paprika

carbs	fibre	fat	protein
0.5g	0g	0g	0.5g

1. Combine all ingredients in a glass mixing bowl.

A great sauce for use in stir-fries and Asian cuisine in general. This sauce is really nice as an alternate sauce for our Pig Candy (see recipe page 42). It takes the little crispy nuggets away from the BBQ taste and back to how we first experienced them, as Asian street food! Ours were warm, straight out of a brown paper bag at a street market; crispy-crunchy pieces similar in size to an almond. We munched on these as we meandered through the brightly coloured stalls, listening to the trade banter in foreign tongues. Big flavours are found in this sauce. Maybe the flavours will stir up warm memories from your days gone by. Enjoy!

HOISIN SAUCE

SERVINGS 24 **SERVING SIZE** 1 tablespoon

- 1 tbsp olive oil
- 1 large clove garlic, minced
- 1 cup water
- ½ cup powdered sweetener
- ¼ cup coconut sauce
- 2 tbsp almond butter
- 2 tbsp apple cider vinegar
- 1 tsp red curry paste or 2 tsp Korean chili flakes (optional)
- ½ tsp coconut flour
- ¼ tsp Xanthan gum
- ¼ tsp cardamom
- ¼ tsp coriander
- ¼ tsp cinnamon
- ⅛ tsp ground cayenne
- ⅛ tsp nutmeg
- Himalayan pink salt, and pepper, to taste

1. Add oil to a saucepan or sauté pan.
2. Over medium heat, add the garlic and cook for 2-3 minutes.
3. Add remaining ingredients and reduce heat to a simmer.
4. Simmer for 10 minutes, stirring frequently.
5. Let cool, then whizz up the sauce in a blender or bullet.

carbs	fibre	fat	protein
1.1g	0.25g	1.3g	0.3g

This recipe is a tip of the hat to one of our favourite burger joints in London.

In 2017, when we were fully dedicated to our keto way of life, we found ourselves in London one more time. This trip was special. It was our first encounter with 'Lights on London,' where they transform London districts with dazzling Christmas light displays. It was also our introduction to the 'fromage-mas'—a tribute to cheese and Christmas, all on one burger. Best part is, it was keto-friendly to boot!

We had eaten Byron's keto-friendly burgers many a time before, but when we tasted this tribute to cheese, we knew we were gonna have to try to create our own version when we had made the trek back home. Picture it: four different types of cheese on the burger AND a little pot of hot cheese to pour over the top! To die for!!

Byron's didn't give us the recipe; in fact, we don't have a clue if our cheese sauce even tastes similar. We do know that your burgers, with just a little sautéed onion and a generous pour of this fromage sauce, will be the best burger you've ever tasted. That's ECKeto-guaranteed!

FROMAGE BURGER SAUCE

SERVINGS 2 cups **SERVING SIZE** ½ cup

This recipe makes about 2 cups of cheese sauce, more than enough for two burgers.

- 4 tbsp butter
- 1 tbsp coconut flour
- 1 cup chicken or veggie broth
- 1 tbsp coconut sauce
- 1 tsp garlic powder
- ½ tsp thyme
- Himalayan pink salt, and pepper, to taste—we used ¼ tsp pepper and ½ tsp salt
- 1 tsp paprika
- ¼ cup 35% whipping cream
- 3 oz cream cheese
- 3 oz old cheddar, Swiss or gruyère, grated
- 1 tsp Korean chili flakes (optional)
- hot sauce, to taste (optional)

1. Melt the butter in a saucepan over medium heat.
2. Whisk in flour and cook for about 2 minutes, until it starts to turn golden brown.
3. Whisk in the broth and reduce the heat. Cook until the broth begins to reduce, 4 to 5 minutes.
4. Add the coconut sauce, garlic, and spices (optional items) and continue to cook until the sauce thickens, about 10 minutes.
5. Reduce heat and whisk in the cream and cheeses. Continue to whisk until cheese has melted completely.
6. Keep warm and give one last stir before serving.

carbs	fibre	fat	protein
4g	1g	30g	2.5g

Try this on steamed broccoli!

I don't think I had one single cooked dinner at Nan's house without having a dollop of Grandmudder's Green Chow on the side. The zesty and spicy tomatoes just added that extra bit of oomph that made a cooked Sunday meal feel special. Years later, I went through brand after brand of commercially available pickles trying to find one that had the proper blend of flavours that I was used to. I kept going back to Nan's homemade recipe.

These days you will always find a few bottles of this keto version of her recipe in my pantry. Come late winter when my reserves get low, I spare them along until the new crop of green tomatoes are ready to go. So, know if you're sitting at my table at that time of year and a bottle hits the table, you should feel complimented. Sharing my last jar of Grandmudder's Green Chow means you're a pretty special person to me.

Cooking time is dependent on the moisture content of the tomatoes you are using and how thick a consistency you like for your pickles.

GRANDMUDDER'S GREEN CHOW

SERVINGS 32 **SERVING SIZE** ⅛ cup

- 2 lbs green tomatoes, sliced and roughly chopped
- 1 large onions, sliced and roughly chopped
- 4 cups white vinegar
- 1 cup powdered sweetener
- 1 bay leaf
- 1 tsp coriander
- 1 tsp garlic powder
- 1 tsp ginger powder
- 1 tsp dry mustard
- ½ tsp allspice
- ½ tsp Korean chili flakes
- ¼ cup Himalayan pink salt
- ¼ tsp cinnamon

1. Place tomato and onion in bowl and cover with salt.

   note **Don't let your tomatoes sit in the salt brine too long or they will become too sour. If you can't get to them right away, drain them, rinse, and refrigerate again instead of letting them sit in the salt.**

2. Cover and refrigerate for 3-4 hours maximum; any longer and the mix will be too briny.
3. Drain vegetables in large colander, rinse, and place in a large pot.
4. Add vinegar, sweeteners, and spices.
5. Bring to a boil over medium-low heat.
6. Cook until the veggies are soft, stirring often.
7. Add water if the chow begins to dry out too much.

This recipe is done to my Nan's (and my own) taste; adjust seasonings to match what your Grandma made, or your own taste.

carbs	fibre	fat	protein
2g	0.5g	0g	0.5g

The term hot and bothered originally meant someone was upset or confused, but in recent years, with women of a certain age, it's a term that has been used to describe the dreaded hot flashes. This keto coach is prescribing this 'medicinal' sauce to all women as a preventative measure, to ward off these flashes. Or at least that's what you can tell your family when you love this so much that you don't want to share. 'Tis medicine for women!

This hot buttered rum sauce is downright decadent. We use this sauce with our Sticky Toffee Pudding, found on page 264. Enjoy! And please, do share.

HOT 'N' BOTHERED RUM SAUCE

SERVINGS 6 **SERVING SIZE** ¼ cup

- 2 tbsp butter
- 1 cup water
- ⅓ cup white or amber rum
- ½ cup powdered sweetener
- ⅛ tsp Xanthan gum

1. Add butter to a saucepan over medium heat and stir until the butter starts to turn slightly brown.
2. Add water and rum, and bring to a boil.

   note **The longer you boil the water and rum the more alcohol will burn off. On average, alcohol simmered in a recipe for 15 minutes will retain about 40% of the alcohol.**

3. Reduce heat to medium-low, and simmer for 5 minutes.
4. Whisk in sweetener and Xanthan gum; let sauce simmer for 10 minutes.
5. Serve warm.

carbs	fibre	fat	protein
0g	0g	4g	0g

These deli-style pickles are fermented in salt and are super yummy. Store them in the fridge, as they won't be canned.

HALF-SOUR PICKLES

SERVINGS 12 **SERVING SIZE** ¼ cup

- 6-8 small cucumbers, cut into spears
- 4 cloves garlic, smashed
- 6 cups cool water
- ¼ cup Himalayan pink or sea salt
- 6 sprigs fresh dill (optional)
- 1 medium onion, sliced into rings (optional)
- 1 tsp pickling spices (optional)

1. Fill a Mason jar with cucumbers; set aside.
2. In a separate container, mix all remaining ingredients.
3. Pour over the pickles and chill.

carbs	fibre	fat	protein
1.5g	0.5g	0g	0.2g

Pickles should be ready in two or three days, depending on how big your cut pickles are.

This crunchy and bright pickled onion is a quick and easy garnish that hits all the taste notes. Just enough sweet, just enough sour...the perfect amount of zing to have on a burger, a pizza, a charcuterie board. Try it. I promise you'll be hooked.

QUICKLED RED ONION

SERVINGS 16 **SERVING SIZE** 1 tablespoon

1 large red onion, peeled and sliced thin

FOR THE PICKLE

- 1 cup apple cider or white vinegar
- 1 cup water
- 1 tsp Himalayan pink salt
- 1 tsp powdered sweetener
- ½ tsp pepper
- pinch nutmeg

1. Combine all pickling ingredients in a small saucepan. Cook over medium-high heat until it starts to roll to a boil. Reduce heat and simmer for 5 minutes.
2. Place the thinly-sliced onions in a Mason jar. Pour the hot vinegar mixture over the top. Top jars off with extra vinegar. Let the onions pickle for at least 20 minutes before serving.

carbs	fibre	fat	protein
0.5g	0g	0g	0g

These pickles were traditionally made by grandmothers across the island, but eventually it became much easier to buy a bottle at the grocery store than to spend all that time bottling/canning. Nothing was as upsetting to the population of Newfoundland as the discontinuation of commercially available sweet mustard pickles in the summer of 2016. It was, without a single doubt, the headline of the year! It was quickly followed by fast-acting consumers swooping in to buy up remaining store stock, only to resell it on 'the Kijiji' for ten times what a bottle regularly cost.

As we're so used to having this as part of our Sunday dinner, we had to learn to make our own. Here is our keto version of that recipe.

SWEET ADORABLE MUSTARD PICKLES

SERVINGS 80 **SERVING SIZE** 1 tablespoon

- 4 cups mini cucumbers, diced (about 12 cucumbers)
- 2 cups small cauliflower florets, roughly chopped
- 1½ cups pearl onions
- ¼ cup salt
- 1 cup powdered sweetener, to taste
- 1 tsp Xanthan gum
- 2 tbsp dry mustard
- 1 tsp curry powder
- 3 tsp turmeric
- 2 tbsp cold water
- 4 cups vinegar

1. Place cucumbers, cauliflower, and onion in a large bowl.
2. Pour salt over vegetables and toss to ensure everything is coated. Let sit 30 minutes, until vegetables are slightly tender. Drain veggies and rinse well. Pat dry with paper towel. Set aside.
3. Dry-whisk together sweetener, Xanthan gum, dry mustard, curry powder, and turmeric in a small bowl. Add 2 tbsp cold water, then whisk again. Set aside.
4. Place vinegar and ½ cup water in large saucepan.
5. Add vegetables and bring to a boil. Reduce heat to simmer.
6. Stir in mustard mixture. Simmer, stirring frequently for about 10 minutes or until mixture slightly thickens.
7. Pour into hot sterilized jars, filling to within ½ inch of the top.
8. Seal with lids and rings. Process for 10 minutes in a simmering water bath.
9. Refrigerate any jars that fail to seal properly.

carbs	fibre	fat	protein
0.5g	0.1g	0g	0.1g

One-quarter tsp of Xanthan gum can be added to thicken the mustard, but our preference is to reduce the mustard sauce by heating.

This jelly tastes so much like a 'not-so-sweet' honey; you can close your eyes and pretend you're a honey bee and indulge. It'll make you a bee-liever!

DANDELION ROOT JELLY

SERVINGS 60 **SERVING SIZE** 1 tablespoon

1. Gather about 4 cups of dandelion flowers.
2. Cut or tear the flower heads in half and place all the yellow petals in a glass mixing bowl, taking care to not select any of the bitter green portion of the flower head.
3. Pour 4 cups of boiling water over the flower petals. Allow them to cool and then place in the fridge for 24 hours.
4. Strain the flowers well and squeeze out as much dandelion tea as possible.
5. Place 3½ to 4 cups of dandelion tea in a large pot—top up with water if you have less than this—with lemon juice and sweeteners. Bring to a boil.
6. Add gelatin to a medium bowl with ¼ cup of cold water and whisk to incorporate. Then whisk the contents of the bowl into the jelly.
7. Remove from the heat and pour into canning jars. Process for 10 minutes with rings and lids in a boiling water bath canner.
8. When processed, remove from water bath, and let cool.

4 cups dandelion petals, stems and greenery removed

4 cups water

2 tbsp lemon juice

1 cup powdered sweetener, or to taste

20 drops liquid stevia

1 packet gelatin—we use Knox brand

if you want a red pepper jelly that will star on any charcuterie board, add the following ingredients to the basic recipe.

⅓ cup red pepper, minced finely

2 tbsp Korean chili flakes

¼ cup apple cider vinegar

note Make sure to strain this red pepper jelly carefully to remove any grit from the pepper spices.

Jelly will be sweeter in liquid form and will lose a little of the sweetness as it cools. Make certain to make the jelly extra-sweet to achieve a proper sweetness level when cool.

carbs	fibre	fat	protein
0g	0g	0g	0g

Cherry Cake is a Pike family tradition for Christmas. I love my new ketogenic health and I don't want for much, but this is one recipe that I really missed dearly, once a year.

This recipe has been a few years in the making. Each year in my ketogenic life, and as the festive season approached, the need to perfect this recipe would rear its head and near about consume me. Suffice it to say, there have been many attempts. Now, don't get me wrong, none of them were horrible...they just weren't 'the one.'

I have found that to perfect the cake I had to go back a step or two and make my own candied cherries. I know it's an extra step and a bit of tomfoolery, but if you're a cherry cake aficionado like me, it's a small price to pay for keto-friendly cherry cake that you can enjoy guilt-free.

HOMEMADE MARASCHINO CHERRIES

SERVINGS 4 **SERVING SIZE** 8 oz bottle

- ½ cup powdered sweetener
- ½ cup water
- 1 tbsp lemon juice
- 2 tsp almond extract
- 1 cup vodka or water
- ⅛ tsp nutmeg
- ¼ tsp cinnamon
- 4 cups cherries, stemmed and pitted

1. Combine sweetener and water in a small saucepan and bring to a boil for about 3-5 minutes.
2. Remove from heat and stir in all other ingredients. Set aside.
3. Fill a Mason jar with cherries.
4. Pour hot syrup over cherries and fill to ¼ inch from the top of the jar.
5. Process in boiling water bath with rings and lids for 3-5 minutes.

want candied cherries? The above recipe is for maraschino cherries, like the ones you would add to drinks. This extra step takes the cherries from this liquid, preserved form to the keto-friendly candied cherries that are used in baked goods, especially at Christmastime.

1. Wait two weeks for the Maraschino Cherries to preserve, then remove the cherries, taking care to reserve the syrup.
2. Place ½ cup of the reserved cherry juice in a skillet over medium heat.

Know your ingredients! Be careful of the sweetener you use here. Some sweeteners recrystallize easily and wouldn't be a good fit for this recipe.

carbs	fibre	fat	protein
13.8g	3g	0g	2g

note **Water can be substituted for the vodka for a non-alcoholic version. Unsweetened frozen cherries can be used in the off-season.**

3. Add 1 cup of powdered sweetener and stir until the sweetener is almost completely dissolved.
4. Stir in the cherries and bring to a boil.
5. Cover and reduce the heat; simmer until the cherries are slightly dehydrated and firm, for about 1 hour, stirring often. You will notice the cherries turn almost translucent as they near being done.
6. Remove from the heat.
7. Allow to cool completely; place on a cooking sheet to dry.
8. Once they're dry, these can be used for baking.

Almond milk can be replaced with water, if you prefer.

Use frozen coffee cubes to replace the ice cubes, if you want a stronger coffee flavour.

Our Islander Ice Capp is the perfect keto summertime drink; it will keep you cool, and give you a serving of healthy fats if you add the MCT/coconut oil.

Hubby Geoff pretty much lived on the brand name version of these during the summer months in our pre-Keto days. He would switch back and forth between regular or skim milk in attempts to make his drink healthier, never realizing the fat wasn't the bad guy. Now that we know that both those options are loaded with sugar and neither recommended, we spent many a sunny Saturday working towards a ketofied version. Islander Ice Capp is the end result of all our trials. We hope you enjoy them as much as we do.

ISLANDER ICED CAPPUCCINO

SERVINGS 2 **SERVING SIZE** 1½ cups

- 2 cups espresso or very strong coffee, cold
- 8 ice cubes
- ½ cup almond milk
- ¾ cup 35% whipping cream
- 2 tsp cocoa powder
- 1 tsp MCT or coconut oil (optional)
- 1 tsp vanilla extract
- 1 tsp powdered sweetener, to taste
- dash salt
- ⅛ to ¼ tsp Xanthan gum

1. Throw all ingredients into a blender and pulse. Serve in your favorite mug, and enjoy!

carbs	fibre	fat	protein
2g	1g	14g	1.5g

The Caproic (C6) acid in MCT is known to cause a tingle or burn in the throat for some people. If this is you, use coconut oil instead.

While the rest of the world celebrates St. Patrick's Day, here on the Rock we take it a step further. Here, where many of us still speak with undertones of Irish brogue, and our hills look like those that grace the cover of *Ireland Today*, it's often Paddy's Week, or at the very least, Paddy's Weekend. Beer is green, the public houses are full and there is laughter and mischief in the air.

Our Irish shake is a nod to St. Patrick, patron saint of Ireland. With or without the optional cocoa, you will love this minty-fresh meal replacement.

Add 2 tbsp cocoa to the blender for a chocolatey-minty drink!

PADDY'S IRISH SHAKE

SERVINGS 2 **SERVING SIZE** 1 cup

1 cup almond milk
1 cup ice cubes
⅔ cup 35% whipping cream
2 oz cream cheese
¼ to ½ avocado
10 fresh mint leaves
3 tbsp powdered sweetener
1 tbsp coconut cream
2 drops peppermint oil
pinch Himalayan pink or sea salt
35% whipping cream, whipped for topping (optional)
1 tbsp MCT oil (optional)

1. Blend all ingredients in a blender and enjoy! Add a whipped cream topping as an option, or stir in a spoonful of MCT oil for added richness.

note Nutrition calculated without optional ingredients for topping.

carbs	fibre	fat	protein
7g	2.5g	48g	5g

We've noticed the keto world gobbling up the 'fathead dough' recipes out there, but just can't get our head around that name. We've been working so hard to be healthy, and over the years have had to endure so much fat-shaming, that the name just doesn't have a place in our lives.

In honour of our progress and our hopes for positive headspace, we've named our version Skinny Face Pizza Crust. We hope you love it.

note **This recipe makes 3 x 9-inch crusts, with 6 slices/2 servings per pizza.**

SKINNY FACE PIZZA CRUST

SERVINGS 18 **SERVING SIZE** 2 slices

One 450g block of pizza mozzarella, shredded

- 2 cups almond flour
- 2 tsp garlic powder
- 1½ tsp cream of tartar
- ¾ tsp baking soda
- ¾ tsp Xanthan gum
- 4 large eggs

1. Shred cheese and set aside.
2. Combine all dry ingredients.
3. Add dry mixture to the cheese and toss to coat all the cheese with the dry mix.
4. Add eggs and thoroughly combine.
5. Use ¼ to ½ cup extra flour if dough is too tacky.
6. Rest the dough in the refrigerator for at least 15 minutes.
7. Form into discs and use hands to shape the crust.
8. Bake at 350°F for 10 minutes, then flip and cook for another 10, then add toppings to pizza and bake long enough for cheese to melt.

Check out our East Coast Keto YouTube channel for the video for this recipe! It shows you how to edge the pizza crust with your hands for a finished look!

carbs	fibre	fat	protein
4g	1.4g	14g	10g

This recipe pairs well with keto crackers, but can also be pressed into service with veggies on a charcuterie board. This is a decadent and rich dip that's an easy-to-make crowd-pleaser. Serve this one to your non-keto friends...unless you think it's too good to share, that is!

SMOKED SALMON DIP

SERVINGS 36 **SERVING SIZE** 1 tablespoon

- 8 oz cream cheese, at room temperature
- 4 ounces smoked salmon, rough chopped
- ¼ cup sour cream
- ¼ cup keto mayo (see recipe on page 227 in our first book)
- 2 tbsp capers
- 1 tbsp apple cider vinegar
- 1 tsp fresh parsley or dill, chopped
- 1 tsp chives, chopped
- ½ tsp Korean chili flakes
- ½ tsp garlic powder

salt and pepper, to taste

1. Place all ingredients in a food processor and pulse to blend.
2. Remove from blender and chill.
3. Either spoon into a mold, or form into a ball with your hands.
4. Sprinkle a little parsley and chili flakes over the top to add to the presentation.

carbs	fibre	fat	protein
0.6g	0g	4g	1.3g

The dedication to the labour of love that is East Coast Keto was tested in a big way while trying to perfect this recipe. It was attempted in many different versions, many different times. All were a resounding flop. I can usually repurpose flops into family-style/not so pretty-looking rejects: failed bread into French toast or keto-friendly croutons; ugly cookies into a crumb to sprinkle on fluff; broken chocolate bark into a think-on-your-feet and act-fast, dense chocolate cake...

...but these were just a NO: straight to the trash bin. Each and every time.

Angels sang when I finally perfected this recipe. As we worked our successful dough and discovered how versatile this dough really can be, we were even more pleased with the possibilities: wontons, ravioli, wraps, fajitas, gnocchi. Delightful!

WRAPS, WONTONS, AND FINE PASTRY

SERVINGS are dependent on how big you make your wraps. For example, a ravioli wrapper would be smaller than a wrap for burritos. Please make your own calculations based on how you divide this recipe in your own kitchen.

- 1 cup almond flour
- 3 tbsp coconut flour
- 2 tsp Xanthan gum
- ½ tsp cream of tartar
- ¼ tsp baking soda
- ⅛ tsp Himalayan pink salt
- 2 tsp apple cider vinegar
- 1 egg
- 1 tsp water

1. Mix all dry ingredients together.
2. Add egg, water and vinegar and use a spatula to start working the dry and wet ingredients together. The more you smash this together, the better your dough will be.
3. Once ingredients are worked together, knead the dough with your hands for about 5 minutes. Really push this dough, like Nan used to way back when, then form into a ball.
4. Wrap the ball with plastic wrap and refrigerate for at least 15 minutes.
5. Roll out the dough and use for your preferred application. We use these in many of our favourite recipes, including beef burritos, chicken chimichangas, and our ravioli. You can find the full recipes in this book.

note Nutritional values are for the entire recipe and serving sizes will depend on how many wraps, wontons, or pastries are made in your kitchen.

carbs	fibre	fat	protein
49g	26g	91g	45g

An Extra Boost

While we don't recommend guzzling bacon juice, knowing that healthy fats help to keep you satisfied will help you manage hunger. Your fat macro isn't one that you have to meet every day; use only what your body tells you it needs, through hunger.

On days that you're active and busy, your body will need more fuel. Make use of the extra fats here by incorporating them into your meals and snacks. On your Netflix-and-chill days, your body won't be as hungry and that's ok! Use less fats on those days. Get in tune with yourself and learn to listen to your body.

Use these fat bombs as a once-in-a-while treat and for an extra boost for your fat and macros. Store them in the freezer and only take out one at a time, to avoid over-indulging.

FAT BOMBS

Bobbi's Chocolate Orange | 217

Cinnamon Bites | 218

Herbes de Provence Bombs | 221

Italian Lemon Fat Bombs | 222

Macaroon Fat Bombs | 225

Peppermint After-Dinner Bites | 226

Pizza Fat Bombs | 229

Salmon Roll-Ups | 230

All macro counts given are per serving.

Like those chocolate-orange Christmastime treats? This is my version, ketofied. You're gonna absolutely love them!

BOBBI'S CHOCOLATE ORANGE

SERVINGS 16 **SERVING SIZE** 1 bomb

FOR THE FILLING

- 8 oz cream cheese, room temperature
- 4 oz butter or solid coconut oil, room temperature
- 3 oz 35% whipping cream
- ½ cup coconut flour
- 2 to 3 tbsp powdered sweetener, or to taste
- ¼ tsp orange essence or 2-3 drops food-grade orange essential oil

FOR THE CHOCOLATE SHELL

- 5 oz Baker's chocolate
- 2 tbsp solid coconut oil
- 1 tbsp powdered sweetener

1. Mix all filling ingredients together in a medium-size mixing bowl and refrigerate for at least 30 minutes.

   note **These fat bombs must be cold after step 1.**

2. Remove from the fridge and using a mini-ice cream scoop, make balls and place them on a parchment-lined cookie sheet.
3. Place in the freezer for at least an hour.
4. Melt chocolate, coconut oil, and sweetener together in a double boiler; mix until smooth.
5. Remove the bombs from freezer. Dip into melted chocolate one at a time using a fork; tap off excess chocolate. Place on parchment-lined cookie sheet, or set to drain using a wire rack.

   note **If using a wire rack, make certain to move the chocolates before they dry completely, as the cooled chocolate will stick to the rack.**

6. Transfer to a refrigerator for 30 minutes.
7. Keep refrigerated.

Use unflavoured coconut oil.

Orange-flavoured water enhancer can be used instead of orange oil/essence.

carbs	fibre	fat	protein
5g	3g	15g	3g

We tested a variation of these delightful little cinnamon nibbles at the local night market in our East Coast Keto food stall. We knew they were going to be successful with the crowd, but man, were we ever surprised at how popular they were!

Instead of our ECK Family asking for a single package of these fat bombs, they were buying them by the case load. Everybody wanted to know the inside scoop on how to make them. Wait no more, lovely family members; here is the recipe.

CINNAMON BITES

SERVINGS 16 **SERVING SIZE** 1 bomb

- 8 oz cream cheese, room temperature
- 4 oz butter or solid coconut oil, room temperature
- 3 oz 35% whipping cream
- ½ cup coconut flour
- 2 to 3 tbsp powdered sweetener, or to taste
- 1 tsp cinnamon
- pinch nutmeg
- 2 tsp vanilla

1. Mix all ingredients together and refrigerate for at least 30 minutes.
2. Scoop into silicon mold or into mini-muffin liners.
3. Store in the fridge or freezer.

carbs	fibre	fat	protein
3g	1.3g	13g	2g

Use unflavoured coconut oil.

Amp it up! Make a coating mix by combining cinnamon and powdered sweetener. Roll the bites into the coating mix.

It's weird to eat flowers, right? I think it's just because we're not used to it. So many plants that grow in our garden are edible, but we just don't know it. Lavender is one of those foods. In my opinion it's such a pleasure to eat foods that you cultivate yourself from a seed and grow in your own yard, especially when we're living in a time full of food uncertainties. I want to know where my food comes from. How about you?

This recipe is a dazzling combination of savory and sweet, inspired by the lavender fields of France. You can buy *herbes de Provence* anywhere that sells finer spice blends, or you can use the recipe found at the back of our first book to make your own.

HERBES DE PROVENCE BOMBS

SERVINGS 32 **SERVING SIZE** 1 bomb

- 8 oz cream cheese, room temperature
- 4 oz butter or solid coconut oil, room temperature
- 3 oz 35% whipping cream
- 3 tbsp powdered sweetener, or to taste
- 1 tsp vanilla
- ¼ tsp peppermint essence or 2-3 drops food-grade peppermint essential oil
- 1 tbsp herbes de Provence mix

1. Mix all ingredients together and refrigerate for at least 30 minutes.
2. Scoop into silicon mold or into mini-muffin liners.
3. Store in the fridge or freezer.

Use unflavoured coconut oil.

carbs	fibre	fat	protein
1.5g	0.5g	7g	1g

Lemon-flavoured water enhancer can be used instead of lemon oil/essence.

It's after dinner. We're at the cutest little Italian restaurant in the underbelly of London. Because space is at such a premium in the city, many restaurants go below street level for their kitchens, and sometimes even their dining rooms. Such was the case here.

Memories of lounge-lizard singers with duck-tailed pompadours, marinara meatballs, freshly made Caesar salad and afterwards, a glass of limoncello: a lemony-sweet liqueur that is a customary drink after a meal in Italy. We don't indulge in the limoncello anymore, but there's no reason why we can't enjoy a lemon-flavoured treat. This is a refreshing limoncello-inspired fat bomb.

ITALIAN LEMON FAT BOMBS

SERVINGS 16 **SERVING SIZE** 1 bomb

8 oz cream cheese, room temperature

4 oz butter or solid coconut oil, room temperature

3 oz 35% whipping cream

½ cup coconut flour

2 to 3 tbsp powdered sweetener, or to taste

1 tsp cinnamon

pinch nutmeg

2 tsp vanilla

1. Mix all ingredients together and refrigerate for at least 30 minutes.
2. Scoop into silicon mold or into mini-muffin liners.
3. Store in the fridge or freezer.

Use unflavoured coconut oil.

Amp it up!! Mix ¼ cup powdered sweetener, zest of 1 lemon and ⅛ tsp salt in a small bowl. Roll the lemon balls in the mix and enjoy!

carbs	fibre	fat	protein
3g	1.25g	13g	2g

Traditional macaroons are small coconut-based cookies. If you like them, I promise that you're gonna absolutely adore these fat bombs. So much so, that you're definitely gonna have to tuck them into the freezer for safe keeping. You have been warned!

These were such a surprise for us both! Neither of us like coconut, but we absolutely LOVE these. Try them, and you will understand why.

MACAROON FAT BOMBS

SERVINGS 16 **SERVING SIZE** 1 bomb

- 8 oz cream cheese, room temperature
- 4 oz butter or solid coconut oil, room temperature
- 3 oz 35% whipping cream
- ½ cup coconut, finely shredded
- ¼ cup coconut flour
- 3 tbsp powdered sweetener, or to taste
- 2 tsp vanilla

FOR THE CHOCOLATE DRIZZLE

- 5 oz Baker's chocolate
- 2 tbsp solid coconut oil
- 1 tbsp powdered sweetener

1. Mix all ingredients together and refrigerate for at least 30 minutes.
2. Scoop into balls or pipe onto parchment-paper lined tray.
3. Place in the freezer for at least an hour.
4. Melt chocolate, coconut oil, and sweetener together in a double boiler; mix until smooth.
5. Remove macaroons from freezer. Drizzle chocolate over the top of the macaroons and place on parchment or set to drain using a wire rack.

   note **If using a wire rack, make certain to move the chocolates before they dry completely, as the cooled chocolate will stick to the rack.**
6. Transfer to a refrigerator for 30 minutes, then enjoy.

Use unflavoured coconut oil.

These are best kept frozen and thawed as you want to eat them.

carbs	fibre	fat	protein
5g	2g	19g	3g

A minty cool after-dinner fat bomb. Mints have the added benefit of helping to settle the belly, so these fat bombs are good for us. Enjoy one after supper! We recommend keeping them in the freezer and take one out as you want to use them.

PEPPERMINT AFTER-DINNER BITES

SERVINGS 16 **SERVING SIZE** 1 bomb

- 8 oz cream cheese, room temperature
- 4 oz butter or solid coconut oil, room temperature
- 3 oz 35% whipping cream
- ½ cup coconut flour
- 2-3 tbsp powdered sweetener, or to taste
- 2 tsp vanilla
- ¼ tsp peppermint essence or 2-3 drops food-grade peppermint essential oil

FOR THE CHOCOLATE SHELL

- 5 oz Baker's chocolate
- 2 tbsp solid coconut oil
- 1 tbsp powdered sweetener

1. Mix all ingredients together and refrigerate for at least 30 minutes.
2. Scoop into silicon mold or into mini-muffin liners.
3. Place in the freezer for at least an hour.
4. Melt chocolate, coconut oil and sweetener together in a double boiler and mix until smooth. Remove fat bombs from freezer. Dip into melted chocolate one at a time using a fork, tap off excess chocolate and place on parchment-lined cookie sheet or set to drain using a wire rack.

   note If using a wire rack, make certain to move the chocolates before they dry completely, as the cooled chocolate will stick to the rack.
5. Transfer to a refrigerator for 30 minutes.

carbs	fibre	fat	protein
5.6g	3g	19g	3g

Use unflavoured coconut oil.

Amp it up!! Add 2 tbsp cocoa to the filling for a chocolatey-minty bomb.

Fat bombs don't have to be sweet; if savoury is your jam, we've got you covered. These savoury one-bite bombs freeze well! Make a big batch and take 'em out as needed.

These are great warm or cold!

PIZZA FAT BOMBS

SERVINGS 12 **SERVING SIZE** 1 bomb

- 12 prosciutto pieces, pepperoni slices, or salami slices
- ¾ cup mozzarella, grated
- 12 tsp of homemade marinara sauce—any marinara can be used, but we prefer ours (see recipe on page 232 in our first book)
- 6 basil leaves, shredded, for garnish

OPTIONAL FIXIN'S

chicken, cubed

bacon, chopped

tomato, diced

sausage, crumbled

mushroom, diced

black olives

1. Preheat the oven to 400°F.
2. Spray a 12-cup muffin pan with non-stick cooking spray.

   note We use a refillable oil sprayer instead of the commercially available oil sprays.
3. Cut each piece of prosciutto three ways to the middle (as shown) and fold the slices partially over on themselves to make a cup that slips into the bottom of a silicon mini-muffin cup. Bake the empty cups for 5 minutes.
4. Place about 1 tsp of marinara and any fixin's into each cup. Top with a spoonful of mozzarella, more or less depending on how cheesy you like it.
5. Return to oven for 5-10 minutes, until the cheese on top is bubbly and the meat is crispy around the edges.
6. Remove from oven, sprinkle basil leaves over the top, and let cool slightly as the cheese will be very hot.

   note Don't bake the fresh basil; sprinkle it on after the bombs are cooked.

note Nutrition does not include optional fixin's and will vary depending on type of meat used.

carbs	fibre	fat	protein
0.25g	0g	6g	10g

A decadent savoury fat bomb that is packed with Omega-3s and flavour.

SALMON ROLL-UPS

SERVINGS 12 **SERVING SIZE** 1 slice

8 oz cream cheese, room temperature

2 tbsp green onion tops, chopped, reserve white part for garnish or a future dish

1 tsp thyme, rosemary, or dill—we use a combination of the three

2 dashes hot sauce

½ tsp salt

¼ tsp pepper

pinch nutmeg

½ lb smoked salmon slices

FOR GARNISH

white bottoms of onion, minced (optional)

1 tbsp capers (optional)

carbs	fibre	fat	protein
1g	0g	10g	10g

1. Combine all ingredients except salmon in a mixing bowl. Set in the fridge to cool for at least 15 minutes.
2. Lay out a large piece of plastic wrap.
3. Overlap the salmon slices, creating a layer 6 inches by 12 inches, with one of the longest sides facing you.
4. Spread the cream cheese mix on top of the salmon.
5. Carefully roll up the salmon, jelly-roll style, and seal the plastic wrap tightly around the roll.

6. Refrigerate until firm, at least 30 minutes, or place in the freezer for 10 minutes.
7. Using a sharp knife, cut the roll into 12 to 16 half-inch-thick slices.
8. Sprinkle with onion and capers, if using, and serve.

Sweet Treats

Most of us sure love our sweets, don't we! Keep these as a treat, though, and not an everyday choice. When we were growing up, dessert was something that happened after a Sunday meal, or a special occasion such as a birthday or Christmas. That's a great example to follow.

Although they're all keto-friendly, eating any dessert every day could be too much of a good thing. Keep them for special occasions in your life!

DESSERTS

Bakeapple Thumbprint Cookie | 234
Cherry Clafoutis | 237
Chocolate Lover's Cheesecake | 238
Coconut Cream Cheesecake | 240
Cream Cheese Chocolate Chip Cookies | 243
Fruit Explosion Muffins | 244
Gingerbread Cake | 247
Keto Turtle Clusters | 248
Lemon Squares | 251
Orange Cream Cake | 252
Partridgeberry Lemon Loaf | 254
Pistachio Ice Cream | 256
Pumpkin Spice Mini Loaves | 258
Saskatoon Berry Custard Pie | 260
Shortbread Blackcurrant Crumble Bars | 262
Sticky Toffee Pudding | 264
Sylvia's Cherry Cake | 266
White Forest Cake | 268

All macro counts given are per serving.

Bakeapple Thumbprint Cookie is another dish that takes me back to my grandmother's kitchen. This was probably one of the first dishes I got my own hands into: standing at Nan's side, getting a hands-on lesson on how to roll the cookie dough into balls and then squish your thumb down into the ball to make a hollow for the jam to fill. Seemed like so much fun back then!

I wasn't a fan of bakeapples at that age, so Nan always made some with raspberry or strawberry just for me. I'm not sure how much of the dough that I worked with back then made it into the oven—I'm pretty sure most of it ended up in my mouth, uncooked, instead!

Bakeapple Thumbprint Cookies is a great recipe to share with the little people in your life to get them hooked on cooking and healthy eating.

BAKEAPPLE THUMBPRINT COOKIE

SERVINGS 16 **SERVING SIZE** 1 cookie

- 2 oz cream cheese, room temperature
- 2 oz butter, softened
- 1 tsp vanilla extract
- 3 tbsp powdered sweetener
- 1 medium egg
- 1½ cups almond flour
- ⅓ cup bakeapples

Bakeapples are not apples; they are a berry native to Newfoundland and other cooler climates. It is also known as cloudberry. Any berry may be used instead of bakeapples.

carbs	fibre	fat	protein
3.1g	1.1g	9.4g	2.9g

1. Preheat oven to 350°F.
2. Mix the cream cheese, butter, vanilla, and sweetener until smooth.
3. Mix in the egg.
4. Mix in almond flour.
5. Wrap dough in plastic wrap and place it in the fridge for 20 minutes to cool.
6. Roll the cold dough into small balls in your hands and place on a baking sheet lined with parchment paper.
7. Press a round-bottomed measuring spoon, or your thumb, into the middle of each ball to form an indentation. It helps to dip the spoon into hot water between imprints.
8. Fill each indentation with bakeapple; don't overfill.
9. Chill the dough one more time.

   note **Cooling the batter before baking helps the cookie to not overspread.**

10. Bake for 15 minutes or until lightly browned.
11. Let cookies cool before lifting them from the baking sheet.

Clafoutis sounds all fancy and intimidating, doesn't it? I'll bet dollars to (keto-friendly) donuts that it would really demystify the dish if I told you it was a baked custard with berries. Call it what you will, this dessert is downright delicious!

A traditionalist would argue that a real clafoutis is made with cherries that have the pits/stones still intact, as it adds a hint of almond to the dish. Our keto version has cherries that are pitted and cut in half for ease of eating, and also to keep the carb value down.

Stone fruit doesn't usually grace the list of go-to fruits on a ketogenic diet, but in reality, cherries are 12g carbs per 100g, which is very comparable to raspberries, strawberries, and other members of the berry family. So, go ahead and indulge. As with any berries, enjoy in moderation and easy does it. It's easy to over-consume and spike your blood sugars on such yummy keto-friendly sweets. This is a 'little dab will do ya' type of dessert.

This recipe sparks a very happy memory for us, one of warm nights, champagne and a very tall tower that sparkles in the night. We hope it helps to make you many happy memories as well. *Vive Paris*!

berries in moderation

In the keto world, our goal is to keep a low and even blood-glucose level all day long. Too many berries would be too much natural sweetness at one sitting, and would raise your blood glucose levels. This could be to the detriment of your state of ketosis.

CHERRY CLAFOUTIS

SERVINGS 6 **SERVING SIZE** ½ a clafoutis

- 1 tbsp butter or keto-friendly oil
- cherries, halved—enough to line the bottom of your cooking pans; we used 6 each per clafoutis
- ⅔ cup almond flour
- ¼ cup powdered sweetener
- ½ tsp cream of tartar
- ¼ tsp baking soda
- pinch salt
- 2 eggs
- ¾ cup 35% whipping cream
- 1 tsp vanilla extract
- powdered sweetener, to dust

1. Preheat the oven to 350°F.
2. Grease three 5-inch or 6-inch pans and arrange cherries along the bottom.
3. Combine all dry ingredients with a whisk, then cream in remaining ingredients with your stand or hand mixer until the batter is smooth and clump-free.
4. Pour the batter over the cherries.
5. Bake for about 30 minutes, or until fully cooked.

   note **Finished clafoutis should be ever so slightly jiggly in the centre and a light golden brown.**

6. Dust with powdered sweetener and serve.

This recipe makes 3 mini clafoutis; half of one clafoutis equals one serving

carbs	fibre	fat	protein
5g	1.5g	20g	5g

So, what's better than chocolate cheesecake? How about chocolate cheesecake with a chocolate crumb base, creamy chocolate cheesecake filling, and whipped chocolate cream on top? C'mon, what do ya want, jam on it? (This is a well-known Newfoundland expression, where the speaker is saying, "Isn't that enough for you?" or "Is this satisfying?")

This is a super-decadent and creamy cheesecake that will satisfy all your chocolate cravings—no jam required!

CHOCOLATE LOVER'S CHEESECAKE

SERVINGS 6 **SERVING SIZE** 1 slice

FOR THE BASE

- 1½ cups almond flour
- ¼ cup butter, melted
- 4 tbsp cocoa
- 2 tbsp powdered sweetener
- pinch Himalayan pink salt

FOR THE FILLING

- ¾ cup powdered sweetener, to taste
- ¼ cup cocoa
- 4 packages (8 oz each) of cream cheese, room temperature
- 1 tsp vanilla
- 3 oz Baker's chocolate, melted
- 3 eggs

FOR THE GANACHE

- 2 oz Baker's chocolate, chopped into small pieces
- 1 tbsp butter
- ½ cup whipping cream
- ¼ cup powdered sweetener

carbs	fibre	fat	protein
7.5g	2.8g	30g	8.7g

FOR THE BASE

1. Combine all ingredients in a bowl until thoroughly mixed.
2. Press into a springform pan; remember, the springform pan is in two pieces and liquid butter will seep out, so make sure you put another pan underneath to catch any drippings.
3. Bake at 325°F for 15 minutes or until golden brown. Set aside to cool.

FOR THE FILLING

1. Mix sweetener and cocoa in a bullet or blender.
2. Combine sweetener mix with cream cheese, in a large mixing bowl.
3. Add vanilla, melted chocolate, and eggs, one at a time, mixing well before adding the next egg.

FOR THE GANACHE

1. Add chocolate and butter to a small bowl and set aside.

Place a sheet of parchment on top of your springform pan before attaching it to the top section. When attached, trim the edges of the parchment so about ½ an inch hangs out of the pan and also line the sides with parchment. Makes for a super easy clean up.

2. Heat the whipping cream in a medium saucepan, whisking so the cream doesn't scorch.
3. Remove from the burner as soon as the cream starts to steam. Do not boil.
4. Pour hot cream over chocolate and butter and add powdered sweetener. Whisk until fully combined.

PUTTING IT TOGETHER

1. Spoon the filling over the crust.
2. Bake for 1 hour or until centre is mostly set.

   note **There should be the slightest jiggle in the centre when it's done.**

3. Remove cake from the oven and allow it to cool before removing the springform ring.
4. Drizzle/pour the ganache over the top of your cake when it has cooled.
5. Cake can be eaten when cool, but is best when refrigerated overnight.

This is a light-tasting cheesecake with just a hint of coconut flavour. The fine coconut in the filling adds a hint of texture and also adds to the overall coconut flavour of the cheesecake. A drop or two of coconut extract can be added, if you like it super coconutty.

COCONUT CREAM CHEESECAKE

SERVINGS 16 **SERVING SIZE** 1 slice

FOR THE BASE

- 1½ cups almond flour
- ¼ cup butter, melted
- 2 tbsp powdered sweetener
- pinch Himalayan pink salt

FOR THE FILLING

- 3 packages (8 oz) cream cheese, softened
- 4 large eggs
- 1 cup unsweetened coconut, fine shred
- ¾ cup powdered sweetener, to taste
- ⅔ cup unsweetened coconut milk
- 1 tsp vanilla extract

FOR THE TOPPING

- ¼ cup cream cheese, softened
- 1 cup 35% whipping cream
- ¼ cup powdered sweetener
- 1 tsp vanilla

carbs	fibre	fat	protein
5.2g	1.6g	31g	31g

FOR THE BASE

1. Combine all ingredients and press into a 9-inch springform pan using your hand or a spatula.
2. Bake at 325°F for 15 minutes or until the crust is a light golden brown.
3. Remove from heat and chill.

FOR THE FILLING

1. Combine all filling ingredients with a stand or hand mixer.
2. Use a spatula to push the filling from the sides of the bowl as you're mixing to ensure the batter is fully incorporated. Beat on high for 5 minutes, or until all items are creamy and there are no lumps.
3. Spoon onto the cooled crust and level the filling with a spatula.
4. Make a water bath by pouring 1 inch of hot water into a shallow roasting pan. Place the water bath onto the centre oven rack alongside where the cheesecake will be set.
5. Place cheesecake on the sheet next to the water.
6. Bake for 1 hour and 15 minutes, or until the top is light brown and there is a slight jiggle in the centre.

Place a sheet of parchment on top of your springform pan before attaching it to the top section. When attached, trim the edges of the parchment so about ½ an inch hangs out of the pan, and also line the sides with parchment. Makes for a super easy clean up.

7. Remove cake from the oven and allow it to cool before removing the springform ring.
8. After cooling on a wire rack for 1 hour, refrigerate for at least 6 hours before adding topping.

FOR THE TOPPING

1. Thoroughly mix all ingredients with a stand or hand mixer.
2. Spread or pipe onto the cheesecake.
3. Garnish with toasted coconut (optional).

note **Coconut can be toasted by dry frying in a sauté pan until it's golden brown. Cool and sprinkle.**

Wrap the sides and bottom of the pan with aluminum foil when baking to prevent leakage.

If there was ever a failproof way to take us all back to our childhood, it's gotta be found in the good old-fashioned chocolate chip cookie. We step ours up a notch with some added cream cheese; it gives all the flavour with an added boost of creaminess.

These cookies are perfect with a glass of almond milk, a cup of tea, or even as a garnish for a bowl of keto ice cream. You just can't lose with this recipe.

CREAM CHEESE CHOCOLATE CHIP COOKIES

SERVINGS 16 **SERVING SIZE** 1 cookie

- 2 cups almond flour
- ¾ cup powdered sweetener
- ½ tsp baking soda
- ¼ tsp cream of tartar
- ½ cup butter, room temperature
- 4 oz cream cheese, room temperature
- 1 egg, room temperature
- ½ tsp vanilla extract
- ½ cup keto-friendly chocolate chips.

1. Preheat oven to 350°F.
2. In a medium-size mixing bowl, combine all dry ingredients, including sweetener.
3. Cream butter and cream cheese into the dry mix.
4. Beat in remaining ingredients except chocolate chips.
5. Finally, fold in chocolate chips with a spatula.
6. Form dough into a ball and chill for 30 minutes.
7. Remove from the refrigerator and shape into 1-inch balls and place on cookie sheet lined with parchment paper. Make sure to give them space to spread.
8. Use a spoon to slightly flatten the cookies, and return to the refrigerator for 15 minutes.
9. Bake for 8-10 minutes, or until the edges become slightly golden brown.
10. Allow cookies to cool for 3-5 minutes on the cookie sheet
11. Transfer to wire racks and let fully cool.
12. Store in the refrigerator in a sealed container.

Chilling the cookie dough will help to stop the cookie from over-spreading.

carbs	fibre	fat	protein
6.2g	3g	17g	4g

One of my favourite muffins, bar none! I was so happy with the results of this recipe right off the bat, except for how they looked....

The first couple of times we tried these, they fell flat in the pan. It took a while to get that perfect mix of temperature and balanced ingredients to make it good enough to share with you, our East Coast Keto Family. Luckily, they all tasted just like the ones we're used to buying off the shelf, which were absolutely delicious in my books.

So, considering the flops that we created along the way in order to get it right, this is a sacrifice we happily make for you, our fans and readers. Hope you love them too!

FRUIT EXPLOSION MUFFINS

SERVINGS 12 **SERVING SIZE** 1 muffin

- 2 cups almond flour
- 1 cup powdered sweetener
- 1 tsp cream of tartar
- ½ cup baking soda
- ½ tsp cinnamon
- ½ tsp Xanthan gum
- ½ tsp salt
- ½ cup butter, softened
- 2 eggs
- ½ cup 35% whipping cream
- 3-4 drops liquid stevia
- 1 tsp vanilla
- ½ cup strawberries, chopped
- ½ cup blueberries

carbs	fibre	fat	protein
5.7g	2.3g	20g	5g

1. Preheat the oven to 400°F. Lightly grease a 12-cup muffin tin, or line with muffin papers.
2. In a large bowl, sift together the dry ingredients, including sweetener.
3. Cream the butter into the dry mix.
4. Add the egg and remaining ingredients, except berries. Mix well.
5. Fold in berries with a spatula.

   note **We recommend using frozen berries so they don't get mushed into the batter when stirring them in.**
6. Evenly divide the batter into the muffin cups.
7. Bake for 20-25 minutes or until the berries are just starting to turn golden brown.

If you don't have the liquid stevia, slightly increase your sweetener to taste.

These are best after cooling in the refrigerator. If you try to remove these from the pan while they're still warm, they will crumble.

My youth was fueled by many gingerbread cookies. Evenings were often spent with my mother in the kitchen; I was always delighted to help line our little gingerbread soldiers up in rows on the cookie sheet. I was even happier to taste them, fresh and warm out of the oven.

It was only in my twenties that I tasted gingerbread cake, all warmed up and oozing with a dollop of whipped cream. By Gawd, I thought I had found Heaven right there and then. The taste was the same as that battalion that Mom and I laid out on the baking sheet, but the texture was moist and fluffy. That new warm and cakey vibe, combined with the sweet and spice of those original cookies was a memory maker. I hope this ketofied version helps make memories for you and your family, too.

Keto baking ingredients don't stick together the same way as traditional baked goods because we don't use gluten. A Bundt pan will be more challenging to work with. Opt for a flat pan where possible.

GINGERBREAD CAKE

SERVINGS 12 **SERVING SIZE** 1 slice

- 2 cups almond flour
- 4 tsp ginger
- 2 tsp cinnamon
- 1 tsp cocoa
- ½ tsp cloves
- ½ tsp nutmeg
- ¼ tsp allspice
- ¾ cup powdered sweetener
- 2 tsp cream of tartar
- 1 tsp baking soda
- ½ tsp Xanthan gum
- ⅔ cup butter
- 3 eggs
- 1 tsp vanilla
- 2 tbsp olive oil
- ½ cup 35% whipping cream
- 5 drops of liquid stevia, to taste

1. Preheat oven to 350°F.
2. In a large mixing bowl, combine all dry ingredients, including sweetener.
3. Cream the butter into dry ingredients.
4. Blend in one egg at a time.
5. Add vanilla, olive oil, whipping cream, liquid stevia and mix well with a stand or hand mixer.
6. Pour into greased 9-inch regular or Bundt pan and bake for 40-45 minutes, depending on how hot your oven runs.

   note Don't move the cake from the oven right away as the change in temperature may cause your cake to fall flat. Instead, turn off the oven, open the oven door about a quarter of the way and allow the cake to gradually reduce in temperature. I usually remove the cake after about 2-5 minutes with the door ajar.

7. Wait at least 5 minutes before turning the cake out into a plate.
8. Allow the cake to completely cool.
9. Frost the cake with cream cheese frosting.

Remember, if your cake falls flat it will still taste good. Cut it into cubes and top with a dollop of icing. Your guests will think that was your plan all along!

carbs	fibre	fat	protein
5.2g	2.4g	25g	5.7g

Not one single Christmas went by without having chocolate turtles in the house. They were Mom's favourite, and it just had to be a part of our annual festivities. I can still see her now, sitting by the Christmas tree with a giant grin on her face as she bit into a turtle, then purposely stretched it, just to see how far that delicious caramel ribbon would travel before breaking.

Needless to say, I picked up my own liking for these little stacks of nutty goodness very quickly. After all, a girl has to follow in her Mom's food steps, right? Wish she were here to try this keto-friendly version. Mom was diabetic, so I think she would have delighted in all the yummy desserts that wouldn't spike her blood sugars.

Feel free to share this one with the diabetics in your family! They will be delighted with the ooey gooey treat, without feeling ill afterwards.

KETO TURTLE CLUSTERS

SERVINGS 24 **SERVING SIZE** 1 cluster

1 lb of pecan halves

FOR THE CARAMEL SAUCE

- 4 oz of butter
- 1 cup powdered sweetener
- ½ cup 35% whipping cream
- ⅛ tsp Xanthan gum

FOR THE CHOCOLATE TOPPING

- 2 oz butter
- 1 cup Baker's chocolate
- ¼ cup 35% whipping cream
- ¼ cup powdered sweetener
- ⅛ tsp Xanthan gum

carbs	fibre	fat	protein
5.5g	3.1g	27g	3.3g

1. Lay a piece of parchment onto a baking sheet. Place a pile or nest of pecans together for the base of each one of the turtles. We did 24 stacks; your amount will depend how big you like these individual treats.

FOR THE CARAMEL SAUCE

1. Heat butter in a saucepan on medium heat until it comes to a rolling boil. Watch the butter very carefully at this stage for it to darken, and for tiny specks of brown to start to form.
2. When the butter is a light to medium brown, add sweetener, cream, and Xanthan gum. Whisk until the sauce comes together and becomes smooth.
3. Reduce heat to low; let the caramel sit on the heat and do not stir.
4. Allow the caramel to cook for about 6-8 minutes.
5. Remove from the heat and whisk.

   note **Do not whisk until you remove it from the heat.**
6. Allow the caramel to rest and cool for about 5 minutes. This will allow the caramel to thicken slightly.

7. Pour about 2 tsp of caramel over each pile of pecans and then put them into the fridge right away to set.
8. While the caramel is setting, work on the chocolate.

FOR THE CHOCOLATE TOPPING

1. Melt the butter and chocolate in a double boiler over low heat, stirring constantly. Be careful, as the chocolate can burn quickly.
2. Add cream, sweetener, and Xanthan gum, and whisk until smooth and thick.
3. Let cool slightly and pour into a squeeze bottle or a measuring cup with a pouring spout.
4. Pour a few teaspoons over each cluster, just enough to cover the caramel. You can use a spoon to slightly swirl and spread the chocolate.
5. Return turtles to the fridge to set.

These can be stored in a plastic container for up to a week.

Lemon Squares is another dish that takes me back to my past. These bars were a constant in our family, one that appeared most Sundays after a traditional cooked dinner. Back then, they used tinned custard to make the base for the filling, but we all know that stuff wouldn't fit in our keto kitchens, so we make our own.

The lemon in these cookies can easily be swapped out with orange, or even combine the lemon with orange for a bright and citrusy twist. Either way, I'm willing to bet that you and your family will love them.

For an Orange Square, lemon can be swapped out for ½ cup water, essential orange oil and the rind of an orange for orange squares. A little keto-friendly water enhancer will help to add the orange colour, and also boost that orange flavour.

LEMON SQUARES

SERVINGS 12 **SERVING SIZE** 1 square

FOR THE FILLING

- 2 tbsp butter
- 2 oz cream cheese
- 1 cup cold water
- juice and zest of 1 lemon
- 2 eggs
- 2 egg yolks—save the whites for other uses
- 1 cup powdered sweetener
- ½ tsp Xanthan gum
- 2 tsp butter

FOR THE CRUMB BASE

- 2 cups coconut, medium cut
- 1½ cups almond flour
- 1 cup butter, room temperature
- 2 tbsp powdered sweetener
- ½ tsp cream of tartar
- ¼ tsp baking soda
- pinch Himalayan pink salt

FOR THE FILLING

1. Mix together first 4 ingredients in a medium-size saucepan over medium heat until fully combined. Set aside.
2. In a separate bowl, whisk eggs and egg yolks together.
3. Slowly drizzle the hot liquid from first step into the whisked eggs.

   note **Go slowly, you are tempering the eggs. If you go fast you will make scrambled eggs.**
4. When the two are fully combined, add sweetener.
5. Whisk in Xanthan gum a little bit at a time.
6. Return the filling to the saucepan and cook on low heat for 5 minutes, stirring constantly. Sauce will thicken after it cools.
7. Whisk in butter to finish. Transfer to the fridge to cool.

FOR THE CRUMB BASE

1. Combine all ingredients thoroughly. Split the mix into halves and press one half into a 9x13-inch baking pan.
2. Bake at 300°F for 10 minutes.
3. Remove from heat and set aside to cool.
4. Spread cooled filling over the crumb base and top with second half of the crumb mixture. Top layer should be sprinkled and gently pressed onto the lemon filling, not firmly pressed like the bottom.
5. Return to the oven and bake at 350°F for 30-40 minutes or until light golden brown in color. Cool completely in the pan before cutting into squares and serving.

carbs	fibre	fat	protein
3.5g	1.6g	18g	3g

Orange Cream Cake is a bright citrusy orange-flavoured cake with a hint of spice and a delightful cream cheese icing. One bite brings me right back to that delicious frozen treat that we all enjoyed as a child.

This recipe was designed after a special request from a member's hubby, who told us that he would go full on keto if I could make an acceptable orange Creamsicle-flavour cake. Now, us crowd at the East Coast Keto Test Kitchen believe we not only met but surpassed our end of the bargain. I believe it's his turn.

All kidding aside, don't try keto unless it's something that YOU want. For us, it was an easy decision...just like it's going to be an easy decision for you to make this cake, over and over again. It's definitely my new favourite.

While this gorgeous cake has all the taste of that frozen treat, it has nowhere near the carbs. We don't recommend you eat the whole cake, but any ketonian should have no trouble working a slice of this keto-friendly dessert into their macros.

ORANGE CREAM CAKE

SERVINGS 12 **SERVING SIZE** 1 slice

FOR THE CAKE

- 2 cups almond flour
- ¾ cup powdered sweetener
- 2 tsp cream of tartar
- 1 tsp baking soda
- ½ tsp Xanthan gum
- ¼ tsp nutmeg
- ⅔ cup butter
- 3 eggs
- ½ cup 35% whipping cream
- 2 tbsp olive oil
- 2 tsp orange zest
- 1 tsp vanilla
- 5 drops of liquid stevia, to taste
- 4 drops food-grade orange essential oil

FOR THE ORANGE CREAM FROSTING

- ¼ cup cream cheese, softened
- 1 cup 35% whipping cream
- ¼ cup powdered sweetener
- 3 drops of food-grade orange essential oil
- 2 squirts tangerine-flavoured water enhancer (optional)

CAKE

carbs	fibre	fat	protein
4.3g	2g	26g	6g

FOR THE CAKE

1. Preheat oven to 350°F degrees.
2. In a large mixing bowl, combine all dry ingredients, including sweetener.
3. Cream butter into the dry ingredients.
4. Add all remaining ingredients and mix well with a stand or hand mixer.

   note **Batter will be thick!**

5. Pour batter into greased 9-inch pan and bake for 40-45 minutes depending on how hot your oven runs. Cake should just be starting to turn a tiny bit golden around the edges.

   note **Don't move the cake from the oven right away as the change in temperature may cause your cake to fall flat. Instead, turn off the oven, open the oven door about a quarter of the way and allow the cake to gradually reduce in temperature. I usually remove the cake after about 2-5 minutes with the door ajar.**

6. Wait at least 5 minutes before turning the cake out onto a plate.
7. Allow the cake to completely cool.

Keto baking ingredients don't stick together the same way as traditional baked goods because we don't use gluten. A Bundt pan will be more challenging to work with. Opt for a flat pan where possible.

FOR THE ORANGE CREAM FROSTING

1. Thoroughly mix all ingredients with a stand or hand mixer.
2. Frost when cake is cooled, and garnish with a sprinkle of orange zest.

note Wait 'til cake is cold before cutting!

Omit orange components for a vanilla cream frosting.

ORANGE CREAM FROSTING

carbs	fibre	fat	protein
0.7g	1g	8.5g	0.7g

PARTRIDGEBERRY LEMON LOAF

SERVINGS 10 **SERVING SIZE** 1 slice

This loaf was traditionally done with blueberries, but when I was growing up Nan knew I wasn't a fan of those. So, when she was lucky enough to have partridgeberries on hand, she would whip up a quick loaf just for her and me.

The icing is often spread on like a normal cake, but my favourite way to present this to guests is to slightly heat the glaze in a small saucepan and dip the individually cut pieces into the warm icing. The little crumbs and berry pieces that fall back into the icing will only add to the decadence of the dish. I've included both the glaze and the frosting so you can try both. Then you get to decide for yourself which you like best!

note **You can buy food-grade essential oil at any store where quality baking ingredients are sold. If you're using them, make sure to use only a drop; this stuff is super concentrated. I use a 1/8 teaspoon measure to drop the oil into, rather than dropping directly into the batter or frosting, to make sure I don't accidentally add too much to the batter.**

FOR THE CAKE

- 2 cups almond flour
- ½ cup powdered sweetener
- ½ tsp Himalayan pink salt
- ½ tsp cream of tartar
- ¼ tsp baking soda
- ¼ tsp Xanthan gum
- ½ cup butter, room temperature
- 8 oz cream cheese, room temperature
- 3 eggs
- 2 tsp pure lemon extract or 3-4 drops of food-grade lemon essential oil
- 1 cup partridgeberries (or cranberries, quartered)

FOR THE GLAZE

- 1 cup powdered sweetener
- 3 tbsp 35% whipping cream
- ½ tsp pure lemon extract or 2 drops food-grade lemon essential oil

FOR THE FROSTING

- 4 oz of cream cheese, softened
- 2 tbsp butter
- 1 tbsp of lemon juice
- ½ cup powdered sweetener
- 2 tbsp 35 % whipping cream
- 1 drop food-grade lemon essential oil

FOR THE CAKE

1. Preheat oven to 350°F degrees.
2. In a large mixing bowl, combine all dry ingredients, including sweetener.
3. Cream butter and cream cheese into the dry ingredients.
4. Add the eggs and lemon flavouring and continue to whisk until combined.
5. Using a spatula, gently fold in the partridgeberries.
6. Spoon the mixture into loaf pan that has been lined with parchment paper.
7. Bake for 60 minutes or until cake is cooked through and the top is slightly golden brown.

We cover the top of the loaf with tinfoil at about 40 minutes into the cooking, to keep the edges from burning.

carbs	fibre	fat	protein
7.4g	3g	36g	9g

FOR THE GLAZE

1. Sift sweetener into a medium-size bowl. Add cream and lemon extract and mix until smooth. Pour over cake.

FOR THE FROSTING

1. Cream ingredients together with a mixer until thoroughly combined. Use immediately.

note Wait 'til loaf is cold before cutting!

Pistachio is not a common flavour but those who like it seem to absolutely adore the subtle and sweet nutty flavour.

My love for pistachio ice cream comes from my early days and my grandparents' little shop. They had an ice cream cooler, and in the summertime, it was usually filled with the standard flavours of vanilla, chocolate, and strawberry. Every now and then they would get Neapolitan...the good one with the mix of green flavour in there. I learned early on that green was pistachio and I learned that I liked it...a lot. My grandparents owning the place was a definite perk; they often indulged me and scooped a little extra of that delectable and cherished green onto my cone.

Our recipe is pure pistachio, so you don't have to ask Nan to avoid the other flavours. If you are the type to enjoy different flavours, why not make a vanilla version of this without the nuts? One lick of pistachio, one lick of vanilla. Sounds like heaven to me!

note Most sweeteners will freeze ice cream into a solid mass after 3 hours. Xylitol and allulose will keep your ice cream soft. But use caution with xylitol if you have pets. **It's extremely toxic to them.**

PISTACHIO ICE CREAM

SERVINGS 8 **SERVING SIZE** 1 bowl

- 1 cup pistachios, shelled
- water, enough to cover pistachios
- 3 cups 35% whipping cream
- ¾ cup powdered sweetener
- ⅔ cup cream
- 3 eggs yolks—save the whites for other uses
- 5-6 drops liquid stevia
- 1 tsp almond extract (optional)

1. Rinse pistachios to remove any salt.
2. Place the pistachios in a medium-size saucepan and cover with cold water.
3. Place over medium-high heat and bring them to the point where they are just about to boil. Turn off heat and remove them from the stove.
4. Strain in a colander and rinse.

to remove the husks

Place the warm pistachios in a kitchen towel or paper towel and work to remove the remainder of the inner husks from the nuts. Our best method is to just remove the husks by hand, one at a time. The husks will have a slightly bitter taste and the more you can remove from the pistachios, the better your ice cream will taste.

You can whizz the discarded nuts into a nut butter, if you like.

carbs	fibre	fat	protein
7.25g	1.5g	46g	7g

5. Place the nuts on a cutting board and chop them up into small pieces. Smaller pieces allow more flavour to infuse your final dish. We don't want nut butter here, just small pieces of pistachio.
6. Add the cream and sweetener to a large heavy-bottom saucepan over medium heat and whisk as it heats.
7. Turn the heat back to a simmer just as the mixture starts to steam.
8. Add the pistachios to the cream and continue whisking.
9. Simmer for about 10 minutes then remove from the heat. Let cool.
10. Place the ice cream base in the fridge to help infuse the pistachio flavour. Leave it to sit for 8 to 36 hours.

11. Return the chilled pistachio-infused cream to the stove and simmer just long enough for it to steam, then remove from heat and strain through several layers of cheesecloth and a mesh sieve, into a large bowl.

    note **If you prefer a nuttier version of this ice cream some of the bits can be reserved to be added into the ice cream, but your end product may be on the gritty side because of it.**

12. While the warm cream base is still in the bowl, rinse out your saucepan and stirring utensils.
13. Add the second portion of cold cream, the yolks, liquid sweetener, and almond extract (if using) into the now-clean saucepan and whisk to incorporate. **Use no heat yet**.
14. Now very slowly whisk the warm cream from the bowl back into the cold egg mixture in the saucepan. This should be done slowly or you will scramble the eggs. You need to temper the eggs and very gradually get them accustomed to the heat of the cream mixture.
15. Once the two are combined, turn your stove back to medium-low heat and whisk as the base comes back to temperature.
16. As soon as steam starts to rise, remove the ice cream from the heat. Let cool.
17. Place in the freezer in freezable plastic containers. Freeze for three hours and then serve.

An ice cream maker can be used at the final stage of processing. Follow your unit's instructions here.

If leaving the ice cream in the freezer for longer than an hour, remove from the freezer about half an hour before serving.

You know fall is in the air when pumpkin spice is being added to coffee cups, mini loaves, cakes, and pies all around the world. The Pike household is no exception to this; our house has been overflowing with the smells of autumn when we play with new ingredients and create new dishes for the fall.

Our pumpkin spice mini loaves are good any time of year, but there's something magical about them in the fall. Maybe it's part of the pre-hibernation process as we switch gears from hot to cool weather, getting ourselves and our nests ready for the even colder temperatures around the corner.

Either way, throw on a sweater and your best pair of boots and indulge in a keto-friendly pumpkin spice mini loaf. These loaves are sinfully delightful, without all the nasty carbs. They're best served cool, so store them in your refrigerator in a sealed container. We hope you like them as much as we do.

PUMPKIN SPICE MINI LOAVES

SERVINGS 16 **SERVING SIZE** ½ a mini loaf

FOR THE LOAF

- 1 cup almond flour
- 1 cup powdered sweetener
- ⅔ cup coconut flour
- 2 tsp ground cinnamon
- 1½ tsp cream of tartar
- 1½ tsp ginger
- 1 tsp allspice
- ¾ tsp baking soda
- ½ tsp Himalayan pink salt
- ½ tsp ground nutmeg
- 1 cup powdered sweetener
- ½ cup butter, softened
- 4 large eggs
- ¼ cup *crème fraîche* or sour cream
- ½ cup chopped pecans
- 1 cup pumpkin purée
- 1 tsp vanilla extract

FOR THE FROSTING

- 12 oz cream cheese, softened
- ¼ butter, softened
- ¼ cup whipping cream
- ½ cup powdered sweetener
- 1 tsp vanilla

carbs	fibre	fat	protein
7.8g	3.5g	28g	5.3g

FOR THE LOAVES

1. In a large mixing bowl, combine all dry ingredients, including sweetener.
2. Cream butter into the dry mix.
3. Add eggs one at a time, stirring between each one.
4. Add remaining ingredients and mix again.
5. Spoon batter into silicon mini-loaf pans.
6. Bake at 325°F for 50 minutes or until a toothpick inserted in centre comes out clean.
7. Cool slightly before removing from pans.
8. Top with cream cheese frosting when completely cool.

We made 8 mini loaves using this recipe. Bake at 325°F for 40 minutes for mini cupcakes.

FOR THE FROSTING

1. Whip cream cheese until it's smooth.
2. Add remaining ingredients and whip again until totally combined.
3. Turn the mixer up to high setting for the last 5 minutes to help the frosting fluff.

Store in the refrigerator.

We grew up here in Newfoundland knowing saskatoon berries as chuckley pears! They grew on trees all over Newfoundland. We kids had no idea they were edible, although some of the older folks swore they made a great batch of wine. What a lost opportunity from our youth!

Saskatoons look like berries, but are more closely related to apples. They are high in fiber, protein, and antioxidants. The name comes from the Cree language; it's an anglicized version of '*misâskwatômina*' (mis-sack-qua-too-mina), which means fruit of the tree of many branches. We certainly didn't know how tasty they were, or we would have been gobbling them up straight off the branches that grew in our backyard!

Whether you know these fruits as chuckley pears, saskatoons, or service berries—which is what they're called in the US—they make a sensational pie! Though slightly on the higher side of carbs, our solution for our saskatoon berry pie is to mix our pie filling with custard. You get to eat flaky pie crust, sweet saskatoons and creamy custard all in one bite.

SASKATOON BERRY CUSTARD PIE

SERVINGS 12 **SERVING SIZE** 1 slice

FOR THE CUSTARD

- 2 tbsp butter
- 2 oz cream cheese
- 1 cup cold water
- 2 eggs
- 2 egg yolks—save the whites for other uses
- 1 cup powdered sweetener
- ½ tsp Xanthan gum
- 2 tsp butter

FOR THE CRUST

- 1 cup almond flour
- ¼ cup coconut flour
- ½ cup powdered sweetener
- ¼ tsp Himalayan pink or sea salt
- ½ tsp Xanthan gum
- ½ cup butter, cold, cut into small squares
- 2 tbsp vinegar

FOR THE BERRIES

- 1½ cups berries
- ½ cup powdered sweetener—optional; these berries are sweet!
- ⅓ cup water
- 1 tbsp vinegar
- pinch salt
- pinch nutmeg

carbs	fibre	fat	protein
6.6g	2.8g	18g	4.4g

FOR THE CUSTARD

1. Combine first 3 ingredients in a medium-size saucepan.
2. Simmer for 10 minutes.
3. In a separate bowl, whisk eggs and egg yolks.
4. Slowly drizzle the hot liquid from the saucepan into egg, tempering the eggs by whisking.
5. Add sweetener and pour back into saucepan.
6. Whisk in Xanthan gum a little bit at a time.
7. Cook at medium heat for 5 minutes, stirring constantly.
8. Finish by whisking in butter.
9. Set aside to cool.

FOR THE CRUST

1. Sift dry ingredients into a bowl and then add butter.
2. Cut butter into dry mixture with a pastry cutter.

   note **Don't use your hands for this step as the heat from your hands will melt the butter and ruin your pastry.**

3. When all the ingredients are incorporated, sprinkle the vinegar over the top and as quickly and efficiently as you can, form the dough into a ball.
4. Cover with plastic wrap and place the dough ball in the fridge to cool for at least 30 minutes, but can cool for up to 3 days.

5. Remove dough from the fridge and roll between two sheets of parchment paper to desired thickness.
6. Place the dough back in the fridge for 10 minutes to ensure it's cold before trying to remove the top portion of the parchment.
7. Remove from the fridge again and take off top layer of parchment.
8. Place the pastry over the top of a greased pie plate and slowly remove the last sheet of parchment.

   note **We fold any excess pastry under the outer edge to help form a thicker crust/edge for the pie. Use your fingers to crimp the pie edges.**

9. Place pie plate on a baking sheet and then into a 325°F oven. Edges of the crust may be covered with foil for a portion of the baking to keep the edges from getting too dark.
10. Bake for 10-15 minutes or until the crust is just starting to turn golden brown. Don't let it brown to much as it has to bake again when it's filled with custard and berries.
11. Increase oven to 350°F.

FOR THE BERRIES

1. Add all ingredients into a small saucepan and simmer for about 10 minutes. Set aside to cool.

PUTTING IT TOGETHER

1. Combine the cool berries with the custard and place the mixture into the pie shell.
2. Return to a 350°F oven and cook for an additional 20 minutes.
3. Let cool. Enjoy!

Hubby Geoff just LOVES blackcurrants and I just LOVE shortbread, so for us (and like us!) this is a marriage made in Heaven! Any berry can be used here, but for us, the blackcurrants hit those perfect notes of sweet, sour, and decadent to the max! Take these along to your next family potluck; I betcha nobody will even know they're keto.

SHORTBREAD BLACKCURRANT CRUMBLE BARS

SERVINGS 24 **SERVING SIZE** 1 bar

FOR THE FILLING

- 2½ cups blackcurrants
- ½ cup water
- ½ cup powdered sweetener
- ½ tsp Xanthan gum

FOR THE CRUST

- 1 cup butter, room temperature
- 1 cup powdered sweetener
- ½ tsp Himalayan pink salt
- 1 egg
- 4½ cups almond flour

carbs	fibre	fat	protein
7.2g	2.25g	18g	5g

FOR THE FILLING

1. Combine blackcurrants and water in a saucepan and bring to a boil.
2. Reduce heat to medium-low and simmer for about 10 minutes. Remove from the heat and let the mixture cool slightly before the next step.
3. Strain the berry compote to remove all seeds and stems. We used a combination of metal sieve and cheesecloth.
4. Once all seeds are removed, return the berries to the pan, and add sweetener and Xanthan gum.
5. Simmer to reduce/thicken for about 10 minutes
6. Remove from heat and allow to cool.

FOR THE CRUST

1. Line the bottom and sides of a 13×9 baking pan with parchment paper. Preheat over to 325°F
2. In a medium-size bowl, cream together butter, sweetener, salt, and egg until smooth.
3. Add almond flour and cream to fully combine.
4. Press 2 cups of the crust mixture into the lined pan.
5. Bake for 20 minutes, or until the sides are lightly browned. Then remove from the oven.
6. Increase oven temperature to 350°F.

PUTTING IT TOGETHER

1. Spread the blackcurrant jelly on top of the crust, and sprinkle the leftover crust mixture on top.
2. Bake for 25 minutes, or until the top is lightly browned.
3. Make sure to cool completely before taking the squares out of the pan. Pull the parchment paper to remove, then cut into 24 bars.

We wracked our brains trying to figure out how to get that tacky/sticky texture without adding an unwanted flavour to this mix. A traditional sticky toffee pudding is full of figs and dates, but using those foods would serve up way too much natural sugar at one sitting, even if we had the tiniest piece. We knew berries weren't 'the match,' as it would just end up tasting like a berry cake.

We finally settled on tomatoes to boost the decadence in this dish. They don't change the flavour, but enhance the texture immensely and puts the sticky in our toffee pudding.

You can serve this sticky toffee pudding on its own, but it's meant to be drenched in Hot 'n' Bothered Rum Sauce. You can find the recipe on page 196.

STICKY TOFFEE PUDDING

SERVINGS 8 **SERVING SIZE** ⅛ of the pudding

- 2 cups almond flour
- ½ cup powdered sweetener
- ½ cup tomato, skins and seeds removed
- ¼ tsp baking soda
- ½ tsp cream of tartar
- 1 tsp cinnamon
- ½ tsp ginger
- ½ tsp cocoa
- ½ tsp allspice
- ⅛ tsp Xanthan gum
- ⅓ cup butter, room temperature
- ¾ cup 35% whipping cream
- 2 tsp vanilla extract

1. Sift together dry ingredients.
2. Mix all wet ingredients together well.
3. Combine dry and wet ingredients in one bowl.
4. Transfer batter to a wet pudding bag, and tie the top of the bag with butcher string, making sure to leave some room in the bag for expansion.
5. Steam for approximately 1½ hours in the pot, over your Jiggs Dinner.

note If you're cooking this on its own, you can use a commercial steamer, or use a deep pot with a few inches of water in it; use a colander, or other means of keeping the pudding out of the water as it steams. We used a metal colander turned upside down in the pot to keep ours out of the water. Check the water from time to time and top up with boiling water if needed.

carbs	fibre	fat	protein
8g	3.4g	30g	7g

This pudding can be served as a side on the dinner plate, but it's most often used as a dessert, served with a rum or caramel sauce.

You can buy commercial steamers or even bake this pudding, but we prefer the traditional method of using a puddin' bag.

As a professional artist, I've been fortunate to meet many wonderful people. Of all of them, none warm my heart more than the dynamic duo, Sylvia and Perry Howlett from Goulds, NL. I first met Perry, a talented photographer, through a social media contest. Fans submitted a picture in hopes of having me paint my interpretation of it, making a creation of combined art that was a part of us both. Perry's photo was a winner and soon after, I had the opportunity to meet this lovely family (pups and all). I knew right away that I had stumbled across some of the sweetest people on this earth.

What does all this have to do with Cherry Cake, you ask? Great question. Cherry cakes have always been a passion of mine. I frikkin' love them, in particular my grandmother's version. It had the perfect amount of cherries, it was light and fluffy, it was sweetened and spiced just right. What's not to love?!?

We lost Nan back in the early '90s, and while I have tasted dozens of cherry cakes since then, none of them stacked up. There was always something missing.

Sylvia gifted me one of her homemade cherry cakes. I was not only gobsmacked with the gift; I was overwhelmed with emotion after the first bite. It was just like Nan's. IT. WAS. PERFECT. I sat in the middle of the kitchen that day and ate far too much cake, forcing myself to stop only so I would have some for another day.

Thank you and much love to Sylvia for allowing me to keto-fy her recipe. I hope I did justice to this treasured recipe. I KNOW my grandmother would approve.

SYLVIA'S CHERRY CAKE

SERVINGS 10 **SERVING SIZE** 1 slice

- 8 oz cream cheese, room temperature
- 8 oz butter, room temperature
- 2 tsp almond or vanilla extract
- 1½ cup powdered sweetener—we use a monk fruit-erythritol blend
- 2¼ cup almond flour
- 2 tsp cream of tartar
- 1 tsp baking soda
- ½ tsp Xanthan gum
- 5 eggs, room temperature
- ½ cup 35 % whipping cream
- 1 cup of maraschino cherries (see recipe on page #)
- ¼ cup almond flour (for dusting the cherries)

1. Preheat oven to 275°F
2. Mix cream cheese, butter, and extract together in a large mixing bowl.
3. Cream sweetener into the butter mixture.

carbs	fibre	fat	protein
7.4g	3g	36g	9g

Keto baking ingredients don't stick together the same way as traditional baked goods because we don't use gluten. A Bundt pan will be more challenging to work with. Opt for a flat pan where possible.

4. Mix all dry ingredients together in a medium-size mixing bowl.

   note **Sylvia recommends sifting dry ingredients twice to ensure a smooth batter.**

5. Alternate adding dry mixture with egg and whipping cream, mixing well between each addition.
6. Dust cherries with flour and then fold them into the batter.
7. Pour batter into a well-greased Bundt pan.
8. Bake on the centre rack for 1½ hours or until a toothpick inserted into the middle of the cake comes out clean, and the top of the cake is golden brown.
9. Let cake cool for at least 10 minutes before taking it out of the pan.
10. Sift powdered sweetener over the top when cool to create a finished look on the cake.
11. Keep refrigerated and serve chilled. *note* **Wait 'til cake is cold before cutting!**

What do you get for a birthday girl who has everything?

It was a loaded question—what do you want for your birthday supper! The inside joke here is that Geoff and I try not to commercialize special occasions with things of monetary value; instead, we try to focus on sharing of ourselves and our time/attention. Our goal is to try to make every day special. Imagine, Valentine's Day every day, instead of being in love/happy only one day of the year!

I thought hard! The main had to be our Southern Fried Oven Chicken; everybody in our ECK Family knows that's my all-time fave. And then for dessert, I invented it! (Or so I thought.) The White Forest cake—a vanilla version of everyone's favourite, the Black Forest cake. This put us in our favorite spot: in the kitchen playing with our tools/toys and creating that perfect vanilla-cherry birthday cake. We hade a grand day, and the end result was, bar none, the best birthday cake ever in creation in the world. Yes, the whole world. We hope this one makes your celebrations feel super special too!

WHITE FOREST CAKE

SERVINGS 24 **SERVING SIZE** 1 slice

FOR THE FROSTING

- 1 cup 35% whipping cream
- ½ cup cream cheese, softened
- ¼ cup powdered sweetener
- 1 tsp vanilla

FOR THE CHERRY COMPOTE

- 1 lb cherries, fresh or frozen, chopped into pieces, or any type of berry preferred
- ½ cup powdered sweetener, or to taste
- 1 cup water
- ¼ tsp nutmeg

FOR THE CAKE

- 2¼ cups almond flour
- 1 tsp baking soda
- 2 tsp cream of tartar
- ½ tsp Xanthan gum
- ¾ cup powdered sweetener
- ⅔ cup butter
- 3 eggs
- 1 tsp vanilla
- 2 tbsp olive oil
- ½ cup 35% whipping cream
- 5 drops of liquid stevia, or to taste

carbs	fibre	fat	protein
6g	1.5g	19g	4g

FOR THE FROSTING

1. Thoroughly mix all ingredients with a hand or stand mixer.

FOR THE CHERRY COMPOTE

1. Add all ingredients to a small saucepan over medium-low heat. Stir as the cherries cook. Remove from the stovetop when the berries have come together as a thick sauce. Let cool.

   note ⅛ tsp Xanthan gum can be whisked in if the sauce isn't thick enough.

FOR THE CAKE

1. Preheat oven to 350°F.
2. Whisk dry ingredients together in a large bowl, including sweetener.
3. Using a spatula or wooden spoon, cream butter into the dry mix.
4. Add eggs one at a time, alternating with vanilla, olive oil, whipping cream and liquid stevia, mixing well with a stand or hand mixer.

5. Pour into greased 9-inch square or Bundt pan and bake for 40-45 minutes, depending on how hot your oven runs. Cake should just be starting to turn golden around the edges.

   note Don't move the cake from the oven right away as the change in temperature may cause your cake to fall flat. Instead, turn off the oven, open the oven door about a quarter of the way and allow the cake to gradually reduce in temperature. I usually remove the cake after about 2-5 minutes with the door ajar.

6. Wait at least 5 minutes before turning the cake out onto a plate.
7. Allow cake to totally cool before moving on to the next steps.
8. When cake has cooled, slice it in half.

   note You can use a long knife but we just use a long piece of sewing thread or flavourless dental floss. Place floss/thread behind cake, where you'd like to make the cut and wrap around so the ends meet. Gently tug and you'll achieve the perfect clean cut.

PUTTING IT TOGETHER

1. Start off with your first layer of cake and add a first layer of frosting to the top. Make this as thick as you like (you may need extra frosting if you use lots) but we mostly use this as a crumb layer to seal over the cake top and help support the cherries.
2. Next spread about half the cherry compote over the top of the crumb coat, leaving a very thin edge with no cherries on the outside of the cake. (don't go right to the edge).
3. Gently place the next cake layer on top, then a regular layer of frosting.
4. Finish with a layer of cherries over the top.

Keto baking ingredients don't stick together the same way as traditional baked goods because we don't use gluten. A Bundt pan will be more challenging to work with. Opt for a flat pan where possible.

Save the pouring of the final cherries for table-side presentation if you have guests. The cherries oozing over the side of the cake will mesmerize your friends and family.

Mad Mixology

In a perfect keto world, we wouldn't consume alcohol, but we don't live in a perfect world and most of us want to indulge every once in a while.

LIQUORS A general rule of thumb is that the darker the alcohol, the more carbs. So, stick to clear alcohol with no flavouring; you can add your own flavours, and then you know what's in there.

PRE-MIXED Save your money on the pre-mixed cans of drink by mixing your own using carbonated water and liquid Stur or other keto-friendly water enhancers.

WINE Use your liquor store rating—usually 1 is dry (best option), 2 is medium and 3 sweet—to help you choose a dry wine. Prosecco and champagne would have the lowest carbs.

BEER There are beers that are promoted as having lower carbs; for example, Michelob Ultra, Sleemans 2.0, and Coors Light, but because they're grain-based, they wouldn't be considered clean keto.

Also note that your body has to burn off alcohol before it burns anything else, so it may slow or stall your keto progress. Most importantly, your tolerance for alcohol will most likely be drastically lowered, so very easy does it. Always be responsible and never drink and drive.

CAPE BRETON CAESAR

servings 4 x 10 oz glasses **carbs** 0.5g **fibre** 1g **fat** 0g **protein** 1g

This drink takes us back to the Mayan Riviera, Mexico, and to late nights sitting in the warm and sultry Mexican air. There's something about a gentle ocean breeze combined with the tart and spicy flavours of a keto-style bloody Caesar that is perfectly relaxing.

The traditional clam and tomato juices wouldn't be keto, as they're full of fillers and uglies. No fear though, we've got you covered. And for the record, this recipe will work just as well in your Nova Scotian backyard as on the beaches of Mexico!

- 2 cups San Marzano strained tomatoes, or regular plain tomato sauce
- 2 cups water
- 8 oz clam juice
- 4 dashes Tabasco sauce, or to taste
- 8 dashes fish sauce
- ½ tsp pepper
- 1 dash lemon juice
- 1 tsp celery salt
- 1 stick celery, for garnish (optional)
- celery salt for rim (optional)

1. Throw all ingredients except celery stick in a blender, and give it a whizz!
2. Add a generous helping to a glass, and add a splash of vodka for a delish keto Caesar. Replace the vodka with a low-carb beer for a Red Eye!

ECK CHRISTMAS SLUSH

servings 10 cups **carbs** 0.6g **fibre** 0g **fat** 0g **protein** 0g

ECK Christmas Slush is our take on the famous NL slush, which is found in most Newfoundland freezers at Christmastime. This keto version is based on the flavours of a mulled wine, but can easily be switched out for the traditional orange, if desired. Try it our way; we're willing to bet it's going to be a new favourite!

- 1 cup keto syrup (Maraschino Cherry juice, see recipe page #) or dry red wine
- ½ cup powdered sweetener
- 3 cans of lemon-lime Zevia
- 1 bottle (750ml/26oz) vodka or white rum
- ½ bottle (750ml/26oz) white rum or whiskey
- 10 squirts of fruity liquid Stur
- ½ tsp cinnamon
- ¼ tsp nutmeg
- ¼ tsp allspice

1. Mix all ingredients together well and place in your freezer in a freezable container.
2. Freeze until the contents are mostly frozen and slushy.
3. Serve over ice, or diluted with club soda or lemon-lime Zevia.

note For orange flavour, swap out the red wine for white and use an orange-based (liquid version only) keto-friendly water enhancer. Look for stevia-sweetened types, and avoid sucralose here. Spices will add to the orange flavour as well. Some may want to customize, or omit them.

MARITIMES MARGARITA

servings 1 **carbs** 0.3g **fibre** 0g **fat** 0g **protein** 0g

I've got to acknowledge and thank my good friend, Carolyn. She was the one who informed me (and through me, you!) to be super careful with tequila! If the bottle doesn't clearly say '100% agave' it has been mixed with sugar water, which translates into a nasty hangover as well as a boot out of ketosis.

This drink is perfect for a sunny afternoon wobbeldy pop in the Maritimes. Make sure you add the salt rim; it elevates the taste through the roof and helps you get a boost of salt.

2 tbsp salt, in a flat-bottomed bowl
1 tsp lime juice
1½ oz tequila,
⅓ can lemon-lime Zevia
1 squirt of keto-friendly lemonade water enhancer, such as liquid Stur
carbonated or sparkling water

1. Wet the lip/rim of the fancy glass with water, inside and out.
2. Place the very top of your glass, sipping side down, into the salt.
3. Twist your glass around in the salt bed to create a salted rim.
4. Add lime juice, tequila, Zevia and liquid Stur and then top up your glass with carbonated or sparkling water.

MONCTON MOJITO

servings 1 **carbs** 2g **fibre** 0g **fat** 0g **protein** 1g

Like your drinks on the minty side? We've got a cool refreshing mojito, just for you. Don't scrimp on the muddled peppermint. Oils and essences are not gonna have the same satisfying result. Use real peppermint leaves that grow in your own backyard, in Moncton or anywhere else!

FOR THE SYRUP

½ cup water
½ cup powdered sweetener

FOR THE DRINK

2 sprigs of mint, about 6-8 mint leaves, muddled
1 oz lime juice
1 oz syrup
1½ oz white rum or vodka
club soda or sparkling water

1. In advance, make your simple syrup by adding water and the sweetener to a small saucepan while whisking.
2. Boil for 5 minutes while stirring until sweetener is completely dissolved. Set in the fridge to cool.
3. Add all ingredients to a fancy glass and top up with carbonated or sparkling water and stir with a straw.
4. Garnish with a twist of lime!

note We muddle our peppermint in our mortar and pestle, then rinse the mortar down with carbonated water. Add berries (try muddling them in) for a berry-flavoured mojito.

SOUTHERN SHORE CREAM LIQUEUR

servings 20 x 2 oz glasses **carbs** 1g **fibre** 0g **fat** 8.5g **protein** 0.5g

The Southern Shore area of the Avalon Peninsula is known for its Irish roots. They're also known for a wicked cup of Irish coffee up that way. Our Southern Shore Cream Liqueur is great in a cup of warm coffee, or poured over ice all by itself.

- 1 cup powdered sweetener
- 1 cup strong coffee, cold
- 1 tbsp cocoa powder
- 2 cups 35% whipping cream
- 1 tsp almond extract
- 1 tsp vanilla
- 2 cups Irish whiskey

1. Combine sweetener, coffee, and cocoa in small saucepan.
2. Slowly whisk in the whipping cream.
3. Simmer for 10 minutes; do not boil.
4. Remove from heat.
5. Stir in remaining ingredients and let cool.
6. Store in a glass bottle in the refrigerator for up to 2 weeks.

SPANIARDS BAY SPRITZER

servings 1 **carbs** 2g **fibre** 0g **fat** 0g **protein** 0g

We all love a glass of wine, but since it hits us so hard these days, we use a fancy glass and some fizzy water to stretch the drink. Gotta pay tribute to my own home town on this one. This recipe allows us to sip our spritzer at our Spaniards Bay BBQs, and enjoy!

1. To a fancy wine glass, add 2 oz of your favourite dry wine.
2. Fill your glass with lemon-lime Zevia, or carbonated or sparkling water.
3. Throw in a couple of berries to make it all fancy.

Keto AF
by East Coast Keto

APPENDICES

TROUBLESHOOTING RECIPES

All of these recipes tested perfectly in our ECK Test Kitchen, each and every one. Keeping that in mind, some of them are more finicky than others; some are easy-peasy to re-create, while others are a right pain in the butt to get perfect. Just like every other thing in life!

Many recipes will need to be tweaked to your own kitchen to suit your own tastes. It's impossible to do a one-size-fits-all-recipe. We recommend that you try it the way we suggest it once, and then use the extra white space we gave you in the book and write your own tweaks in the margins. Some of us like things spicier, sweeter, or a little different in some way than others. Ovens and stoves work at different temperatures, our homes are at different elevations, and the ingredients we use are just a little different. Here are some tips to help.

If your recipe isn't firming enough: Look and see what you can increase in your recipe. Add more flour, more fibre, more Xanthan, more cream cheese.

If your recipe is drying out in the pan/oven: Add broth or another liquid, reduce temperature.

If your recipe isn't brown enough: Increase heat, broil, sear, or increase cooking time.

If your dough is spreading too much: Chill dough or add more almond flour.

If your batter is too thick: Add more of the liquid used in the recipe.

If your recipe doesn't have enough flavour: Try adding salt first. Up the spices that you used in the recipe, use vinegar (acid) as a flavour enhancer.

If your recipe is too spicy: Try adding more broth and stretching the sauce/soup, add a neutral or cream base ingredient like cream, cheese, or cream cheese, add peanut/almond butter, add sweetener.

At the end of the day, if things don't look or taste perfect, don't throw it out. Most all food can be salvaged. Flopped breads can be turned into keto French toast or croutons. Ugly cookies can be crumbled atop fluff or ice cream etc. Think outside the box and keep your cool.

SEASON TO TASTE—WHAT DOES THAT EVEN MEAN?

Many recipes will contain a direction to season to taste for salt. Here's why!

Most times when your recipe isn't quite right flavour-wise, it's an issue with salt. Try an experiment with a simple batch of broth. Cook it unsalted, and it will taste flat and flavourless.

As you start to add salt a little at a time you will notice notes of more complex flavours that you didn't taste before. Keep adding salt and tasting, until it's just right for you and your family. You'll know it when you hit it. It shouldn't taste salty; it should taste salted and perfectly balanced.

Salt is not just for savoury dishes, it's a flavour enhancer that will add heightened taste to any meal.

COOK INTUITIVELY

Convenience foods have really done a number on us over the years. We have gotten so used to opening a package for dinner, or finding a gadget to simplify supper, that we have almost forgotten the part that separated us from the animals way back when: the ability to make fire and cook for ourselves. Along with this loss came the inability to be intuitive in the kitchen, to use our own judgment and common sense to create foods.

A kitchen is very much a 'think on your feet' environment. Real life cooking looks nothing like the fairy tale often presented on cooking shows. More often, it's fallen cakes, burnt chicken, under-cooked meals and many other culinary disasters waiting to happen. The secret of cooking success is knowing how to respond and react when the unexpected happens.

These are some basic methods that can translate to almost everything you create in the kitchen, and will help you to become a better overall cook.

We've all been led to believe that our ovens are accurate, when in reality they're probably the most inaccurate tool in our kitchen. When you set your oven to 350°F, most real oven temperatures will cycle back and forth between 325-400°F. The front of your oven will be cooler than the back, and there will most likely be hot spots or variations in temperature from side to side.

Learn to watch your food and don't rely blindly on a recipe; instead, rely on your own senses.

Use your eyes. We eat with our eyes before the food ever enters our mouth. When cooking, knowing what to look for along the way really helps the process. Look for colour changes to indicate doneness. Onions will turn slightly translucent, while most fish will do the opposite and become opaque as they cook.

Watch for those golden-brown colours—a crispy crust or the look of seared meat. If the bacon on your bacon-wrapped meatloaf doesn't look done, it probably needs more time.

Cakes pull away from the sides of the pan when they are cooked. Custards and cheesecakes have the slightest jiggle when they're done.

If something is crisping or browning too fast, your temperature could be too high. These visual cues and others can be learned, and will be a great help in getting your food just right.

Use your nose. Try to identify foods by smell! Some are easy, like apple, cinnamon, or garlic, but what about broccoli or tomato? Could you identify them by smell?

Learn the smells you're looking for. Notice how an onion or clove of garlic smells when raw or slightly cooked; notice how the smell changes when it burns. Smell spices as you open them. Familiarize yourself with how they smell (and taste), and it will help you to know which to add to a dish that needs a little extra something.

Use your ears. Pans should be hot before we add oil and other ingredients. In most cases, there should be pops and sizzling noises when you place a meat or vegetable in oil. When the popping stops, especially in deep frying, it's a sign that the water content of the food (especially veg) is gone, and your item is cooked.

Pancakes will form bubbles when they are cooked and need to be flipped.

Learn the difference between a sizzle and the glug-glug sound a pan makes when it has too much oil and needs to be drained.

Turn on that timer!

Use your sense of touch. Meats firm as they cook. Use your hands to tell the difference between the levels of doneness in a piece of meat protein, as follows:

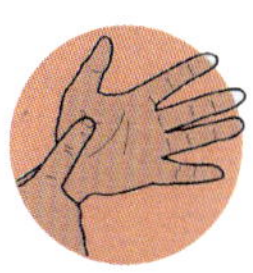

RAW Open the palm of your hand and relax the hand. Press/push into the fleshy area between the thumb and the base of the palm. This is what raw meat feels like.

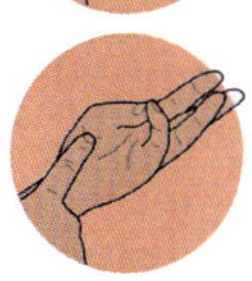

WELL DONE Now press your thumb and pinky tighter and feel the same area again. Well done should feel firm like that.

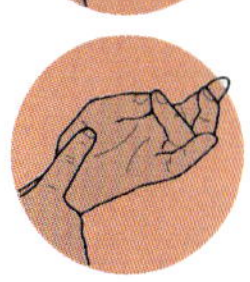

MEDIUM Press your thumb and ring finger to feel; it should be slightly less firm.

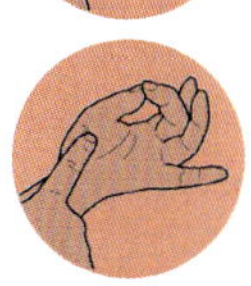

MEDIUM RARE Press thumb and middle finger to feel; this it should be less firm again.

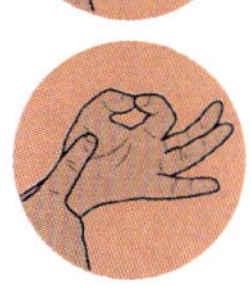

RARE Press thumb and index finger down; this should feel close to how your open and relaxed hand felt.

Use your sense of taste. Taste is 'king of all' in the kitchen. Taste everything you cook, every step of the way, and season every step. Successful cooking happens when you season and taste as you go, not just at the end of cooking.

Even if it's raw pork meatballs or raw cookie dough, spoon out a tiny portion and fry it up fast in the pan to pre-taste a small portion. You will easily be able to tell if your food needs more salt or sweet before you cook the whole batch.

Learning to cook to taste is an important part of your own food journey! As much as we can build recipes and inspire you with our keto creations, we cannot interpret your own likes and dislikes, nor your family'spreference for each taste. Anyone who is used to cooking for a crowd, or on a smaller scale, cooking for a family, will quickly realize that we are all different here. When tasting, consider the five basic tastes: sweet, salty, sour, bitter and umami—yes, there has been a new one added since we all went to school! The foods we eat are most often a complex combination or balance of these tastes, and not just one single taste. For example, a balanced chicken wing will not just be spicy, it will often have notes of salty and tangy-sweet as well. Think of a raspberry vinaigrette; it is a combination of sweet from the raspberry, salty/spicy from the salt and spices, and bitter/acidic from the vinegar. Even basic chocolate is a combination of sweet, salt and bitter. Learning how to harness these flavours for your own family's needs is really a science in itself!

tip

Play with your tastes! Add herbs to something sweet, as you see in our *Herbes de Provence* fat bombs recipe! Add strawberry to your savoury salad, such as in our onion dressing on page 173. Finish the Keto Turtle Cluster with a sprinkle of finishing salt as seen on page 248! Delight is often found in combining our tastes into one single bite.

WHAT TO AVOID

Keto is always 'ingredients first'; before you even look at carbs you need to determine if the ingredients are clean. It's possible to do dirty keto, but you will never reach the optimal health benefits of keto without eating clean.

Specifically, learn to avoid foods that spike our blood glucose level (successful ketonians keep a low and even blood glucose level) and inflammatory foods, which cause a host of problems.

Here is a list of known uglies and what to watch for:

- ✘ **Acesulfame Potassium** Nasty chemical sweetener. Consider it poison.
- ✘ **Additives** Chemicals are not your friend on keto. Avoid as much as possible. If you can't pronounce it, or don't know what it is, chances are you shouldn't eat it if you want to successfully keto. Also avoid preservatives as much as possible.
- ✘ **Aspartame** Nasty chemical sweetener. Consider it poison.
- ✘ **Carrageenan** Food additive derived from algae. Causes gut issues and has been linked to cancer.
- ✘ **Food Colouring** Food dyes have been linked to certain cancers. Avoid as much as possible.
- ✘ **Grains** Of any kind: amaranth, barley, buckwheat, corn, bulgur, millet, oats, quinoa, rye, rice, sorghum, spelt, wheat.

- ✘ **Gluten** Signifies that starch and grains are present, is inflammatory, and causes unstable blood glucose levels. Avoid.
- ✘ **Hidden Sugar** It's not just the white stuff in the bowl. Familiarize yourself with the many names.
- ✘ **High Fructose Corn Syrup** The ultimate in nasty sugars.
- ✘ **Isolate** Usually denotes chemical manipulation. Avoid.
- ✘ **Isomalt** Hidden sugar, avoid.
- ✘ **Keto-Labelled Foods** Those keto bars, drinks, and packets? Treat them as suspect and check all ingredients.
- ✘ **Ketones, Exogenous** Classified with keto shakes, keto coffees, keto powders, and keto pills. Avoid these at all costs. They are not keto! Using these is similar to going to a gym and spraying sweat on yourself to get a workout. It doesn't work that way; you need to make the ketones yourself by restricting carbs.
- ✘ **Lentils and Legumes** Are all inflammatory. This includes beans (except Mung beans), cashews, peas, peanuts.
- ✘ **Natural Flavour** Means it was derived from a natural source, after which they can do almost anything with it. This is an unknown wild card that is in many foods. Avoid as much as possible.
- ✘ **Maltitol** Nasty hidden sugar that causes disaster pants (sudden and unexpected trips to bathroom). Sorbitol is another.
- ✘ **Margarine** Not real food. Use butter or ghee instead.
- ✘ **Maltodextrin** Nasty hidden sugar.
- ✘ **Modified** Usually signals a chemical change made to an ingredient.
- ✘ **Modified + Starch** Often signifies MSG. Known to spike blood glucose levels over 300%. Avoid.
- ✘ **MSG** Monosodium glutamate, a flavour enhancer. Known to spike your blood glucose and cause migraines. Evil.
- ✘ **'Ose' Endings** Any ingredient that ends with '-ose' is a hidden sugar. Avoid.
- ✘ **'Poly' Prefixes** Means 'many', most usually something that is chemically modified to enhance flavour. Likely not a good keto ingredient.
- ✘ **Protein Bars/Shakes** Most are whey-based and full of chemicals. Quality matters in keto. Eat real foods, not replacements.
- ✘ **Soy** Is inflammatory and is also a hormone interrupter that's particularly nasty for women. Avoid!
- ✘ **Starches** Think of starches as super sugars. They spike our blood glucose levels for longer and often higher than sugar. Avoid at all costs.

- ✗ **Sugar Words** Or words that hint at sugar, such as caramel, syrups, coconut sugar, dextrin, molasses, malt, nectar, honey, treacle. Avoid them all.
- ✗ **Veggie Oils** Are not really veggie oils, they're seed oils that are inflammatory. Avoid.
- ✗ **Whey** Spikes blood glucose levels. It is the base of most protein bars, and a large part of the reason why they're definitely not keto.

BUILDING A KETO PANTRY

There is a pantry switchover that occurs when you start keto. We recommend that you slowly ramp up your specialty items instead of doing a whole switch. These things are not requirements for keto cooking and you can keto quite easily without them; they would mostly be considered extra items. Don't forget to research the ingredients for these items when you shop. Even within a brand, there are different recipes with different ingredients. Don't assume because one is keto that the other is as well. Investigate every single product independently each time.

Below is a list of items you may eventually wish to include in your pantry, with our personal recommendations on brands where applicable.

- ✓ **Apple Cider Vinegar (ACV)** May be subbed for any cider vinegar, or alternate vinegar. Found in most grocery stores.
- ✓ **Almond and Coconut Flours** Found in the health/organic section of bigger grocery stores and some health stores, select Bulk Barns, and Costco.
- ✓ **Bakeapple** Berry native to northern US, Canada, Greenland, also known as the cloudberry, nordic berry, and knotberry. Looks like a peach-coloured raspberry. May be subbed out for any berry. This is NOT a baked apple; it is a berry.
- ✓ **Brown Sugar Sweetener** Choose Lakanto Golden, which is a sweetener made from monk fruit. Available in health food stores, and bigger grocery stores in the health food section.
- ✓ **Buffalo Mozza** Round/ball-shaped specialty Buffalo cheese, usually suspended in liquid. Found in larger grocery stores in the specialty cheese section or Costco (two-pack tub).
- ✓ **Celery Seeds** Spice section and Bulk Barn.
- ✓ **Chocolate** Baker's unsweetened and Compliments unsweetened brands. Found in the baking section of your grocery store.
- ✓ **Chocolate Chips** Lily's milk chocolate chips (blue bag) only, found in health food stores. Alternatively, just chip/cut up unsweetened Baker's chocolate.
- ✓ **Coconut Milk** Usually found in cans in the international section. This is different from coconut *sauce*.
- ✓ **Coconut Sauce** Fermented coconut sap, also known as coconut aminos (although most coconut

amino's are NOT fermented and WILL be higher in carbs/sugar). This is a soy sauce replacement that enhances flavour. May be omitted in most recipes. Found in the health/organic section of bigger grocery stores and select health stores and Bulk Barns. This is not the same as coconut *milk*.

- ✓ **Confectioner's Sweetener** Sweetener that can be purchased in confectioner's (powdered) form, or you can grind up granular sweeteners. Many of these sweeteners don't break down the same way as regular sugar, so we powder all of ours as soon as we get them home.
- ✓ **Cream Cheese** Blocks only, not the tubs. Available at any grocery store, or Costco.
- ✓ **Cream of Tartar plus Baking Soda** Use as a replacement for baking powder. Found in the baking section or spice section of your grocery, or at Walmart and Costco. To use: for every tsp of baking powder, replace with ½ tsp cream of tartar and ¼ tsp baking soda.
- ✓ **Crème Fraîche** Can be used instead of cream cheese, clean sour cream and 35% whipping cream in most cases. Can be found in bigger grocery stores, and Colemans. Ask your retailer to carry it if they don't have it!
- ✓ **Essential Oils** Make certain to choose a high-quality food-grade oil, such as LorAnns. Found at Bulk Barn, Colemans, or Michaels, usually in the baking section.
- ✓ **Fish Sauce** A fermented liquid condiment and a flavour enhancer. This is a Worcestershire sauce replacement. May be omitted in most recipes. Found in the international section of bigger grocery stores and some health food stores. You will notice a minimal amount of sugar here, but most of the sugar would be used up in the fermentation process.
- ✓ **Flax Meal** Ground flax seed. Found in health/organic sections of bigger grocery stores, Bulk Barns, and some health food stores
- ✓ **Garam masala (Indian spice blend)** Can include cardamom, turmeric, black pepper, clove, coriander, and other Indian spices, that help to build Asian flavours. Found in the spice section in grocery stores or Bulk Barn. Garam masala may be used instead of allspice in a pinch. For more common spice mixes, see our first book.
- ✓ **General Keto Oil** Use lard, bacon fat, tallow (beef fat), olive oil, avocado oil, coconut oil or other cold-pressed oil. Choose unflavoured and liquid coconut oils for most coconut oil recipes. Found with the oils and vinegars in grocery stores, health food stores, and Costco. Avoid inflammatory vegetable oils.
- ✓ **Halloumi** A specialty cheese from the eastern Mediterranean region that can be grilled, fried or deep fried. Found in the specialty cheese section of larger grocery stores and Costco.
- ✓ **Himalayan Pink Salt or Natural Sea Salt** Usually found in the spice section in your grocery store and Costco.
- ✓ **Keto Products** Commercially available keto bread, crackers, bars, and other similar products should generally be treated as suspect. Please check ingredients for these items at all times. Use the what to avoid list! These products will probably not be real keto.

✓ **Konjac Noodles** Shirataki noodles made from the konjac root of southeast Asia. Found in health/organic section of bigger grocery stores, Bulk Barns, and some health food stores. Read packaging to ensure these are not soy.

✓ **Lard** Found in the baking section of most grocery stores, as well as Walmart and Costco.

✓ **Liquid Smoke** Used for adding a smoky flavour to foods, it can be found in the sauces section of the grocery store.

✓ **Medium-chain triglycerides** (MCT) A type of saturated fat found in many foods, such as dairy products. In the keto community, they are often consumed as refined and separated fatty acids that are derived from coconut or palm oil; these include capronic acid (C6), caprylic acid (C8), capric acid (C10), and lauric acid (C12). Found in health food stores, the organic/health section of larger grocery stores, and Costco.

The lower the number of the fatty acid, the better it is for health and weight loss. Your liver converts MCTs into ketones—the fuel source your body produces when it burns fat for fuel. The shorter the chain, the more quickly it is used by the body. A bottle of MCT oil would be mostly composed of C6, while coconut oil mostly contains the least efficient oil, C12 (lauric acid).

✓ **Monk Fruit** A natural sweetener that is derived from a small round fruit native to southern China, Also known as Luo Han Guo or swingle fruit.

✓ **Mung beans** An alternative to split peas. While slightly high in carbs, it is the only anti-inflammatory legume. Found at Bulk Barn or health food stores, it must be soaked overnight. Should be used in moderation only.

✓ **Newfoundland Savoury** Summer savory, used in Newfoundland stuffing/dressing. May be used in place of thyme or any other green herb.

✓ **Nutritional Yeast** A cheese-flavoured thickening agent that can be added to sauces, stews, gravies, and other savoury recipes. A source of vitamin B. Found in health stores or in organic section of your grocery store.

✓ **Parmesan cheese** Should be purchased in blocks of hard cheese and hand-shredded.

✓ **Partridgeberries** Small red berries that grow in Eastern North America and resemble a small cranberry, also known as lingonberry. Can be swapped out for any berry.

✓ **Psyllium Husk** Found in the health/organic section of bigger grocery stores, Bulk Barns and some health food stores. Do not use psyllium husk from the pharmacy section, as these products often contain additives such as sugar and chemical flavourings.

✓ **Pork Belly** Uncured bacon cut of meat. Ask at the butcher counter of the grocery store for this, or Costco. We recommend 2x4 squares, cut at home.

✓ **Pork Rinds** Look for brands such as Baconets by Frito Lay and Bacon Puffs by Old Dutch.

- ✓ **Red Pepper/Korean Chili** These are interchangeable in recipes. Found in Asian grocery stores or the international section of larger grocery stores.
- ✓ **Salt Beef** A staple in traditional Newfoundland cooking, it is salt-cured beef, similar to pickled cottage roll or American corned beef. Found in most grocery stores.
- ✓ **San Marzano Tomatoes** Any clean canned tomatoes can be used here; these just have a little extra flavour. Found at Costco (in a six pack or a huge can) and larger grocery stores.
- ✓ **Sausage and Cured Meats** It's normal to see small amounts of sugar here; the sugar will be mostly used up in the curing process. Avoid starches here.
- ✓ **Soda Stream** Use only as a source of carbonated water or with keto-friendly water enhancers. Soda Stream syrups are not keto.
- ✓ **Sour Cream** most contain starch, which is equivalent to a super sugar and should be avoided. We recommend Gay Lea Gold, found in Walmart and bigger grocery stores. Crème fraîche can be used instead.
- ✓ **Sweeteners** always check ingredients for sweeteners before purchasing!! They are not all equal. **Avoid** Stevia in the Raw, all baking blends, yellow Sugar Twin, Acesulfame-Potassium, Splenda, and Aspartame. Always check ingredients here.
- ✓ **Veggies** there are a variety of less-well-known vegetables such as daikon radish, jicama, celeriac/celery root, lemongrass, and chayote squash that are keto-friendly and can be easily researched on the Internet. Found in most bigger grocery stores; ask your retailer to carry them if they don't have them.
- ✓ **Water Enhancers** look for brands such as Stur and President's Choice. Buy liquid only—do NOT use powdered varieties, as the powdered form of these brands are not keto. Avoid sucralose, aspartame, and acesulfame potassium in water enhancers.
- ✓ **White Balsamic Vinegar** Tastes like regular balsamic, only with much less sugar. Dark balsamic vinegar is not keto, as the darker colour comes from burnt sugar. Located with the vinegars in bigger grocery stores and Walmart. Ask your retailer to carry it if they don't have it.
- ✓ **Xanthan Gum** This is a keto-friendly thickening agent for soups, stews, gravies etc. Found in the health/organic section of bigger grocery stores and some health food stores and Bulk Barns, usually in cellophane packs.
- ✓ **Xylitol** A sweetener that can be used instead of any other keto-friendly sweetener. Use to sweeten to taste in most cases. Found in health food stores, bigger grocery stores in the health/organic section, and Bulk Barns. **IMPORTANT: Xylitol is extremely toxic to pets**. We won't even bring this into the house. This ingredient is also found in many chewing gums.
- ✓ **Zevia** Sparkling/carbonated water (brand names such as La Croix, Bubly) that is sweetened with stevia.
- ✓ **Zoodles** Spiralized zucchini.

Recipe Index

B

Bakeapple Thumbprint Cookie, 234
Basic Omelette Recipe, 56
Beef Burritos, 122
Big G Sauce, 190
Bobbi's Chocolate Orange, 217
Breakfast Pizza, 59
Broccoli and Cheese Soup, 82
Butter-Poached Cod, 100

C

Cabbage Rolls, 124
Cape Breton Caesar, 271
Cherry Clafoutis, 237
Chicken Chimichangas, 126
Chicken Cordon Bleu, 128
Chinese-Style Faux Fried Rice, 164
Chioggia Beet Salad, 167
Chocolate Lover's Cheesecake, 238
Cinnamon Bites, 218
Clam Chowder, 85
Coconut Cream Cheesecake, 240
Corned Beef Meat Cakes, 60
Crab Cakes, 103
Crab Rangoon, 35
Crab-Stuffed Mushrooms, 32
Cream Cheese Chocolate Chip Cookies, 243
Crêpes with Hazelnut Sauce and Strawberries, 62
Curried Cod 104

D

Daikon Asian Slaw, 168
Dandelion Root Jelly, 203
Dutch Baby, 64

E

ECK #1 Keto Steak Sauce, 189
ECK Christmas Slush, 271
ECK Prosciutto-Wrapped Sole, 107
Eggs Florentine, 67
Embrace Your Saucy Side, 188

F

Farmer's Casserole, 68
French Onion Soup, 86
Frikkin' Deadly Chocolate Granola, 36
Fromage Burger Sauce, 192
Fruit Explosion Muffins, 244

G

Garlic Butter Noodles, 171
Ginger Beef, 131
Gingerbread Cake, 247

Grandmudder's Green Chow, 195
Grilled Calamari, 108

H

Half-Sour Pickles, 198
Ham and Green Onion Chaffle, 71
Herbes de Provence Bombs, 221
Hoisin Sauce, 191
Homemade Maraschino Cherries, 204
Homestyle Chicken Pot Pie, 132
Honey Garlic Spare Ribs, 135
Hot 'n' Bothered Rum Sauce, 196

I

Islander Iced Cappuccino, 206
Italian Crack Slaw, 136
Italian Lemon Fat Bombs, 222

J

Jiggs Dinner Breakfast Croquettes, 72

K

Keto Hash Browns, 75
Keto Turtle Clusters, 248
Kohlrabi and Green Onion Soup, 89
Korean BBQ Chicken, 139

L

Lemon Squares, 251
Lobster Bisque, 90
Lobster Risotto, 111
Lobster Roll, 112

M

Macaroon Fat Bombs, 225
Maritimes Margarita, 272
Miss Bobbi's Snack Chips with Seasoning Blends, 38
Mom's W Sauce Chops, 140
Moncton Mojito, 272
Mushroom Risotto, 41

N

Nanny Wazzer's Chicken Soup, 92
Newfoundland Toutons, 76

O

Orange Cream Cake, 252

P

Paddy's Irish Shake, 207
Pan-Seared Scallops with Celeriac, 115
Partridgeberry Lemon Loaf, 254
Peanut Butter 'n' Jelly Pancakes, 78
PEI Faux-tato Pie, 174
Peppermint After-Dinner Bites, 226
Pig Candy [A Sidekick Recipe], 42
Pike House Italian Salad, 172
Pistachio Ice Cream, 256
Pizza Fat Bombs, 229
Pork Meatloaf with Asian Glaze, 143
Primavera Chicken with Tomato Sauce, 144
Pumpkin Spice Mini Loaves, 258

Q

Quickled Red Onion, 199

R

Ricotta and Tomato Bruschetta, 44
Roasted Crispy Pork Ravioli with Rustic Tomato Sauce, 46
Roasted Rack of Lamb with White Balsamic Glaze, 147
Roasted Red Pepper Soup, 95

S

Salisbury Steak with Mushroom Gravy, 148
Salmon Roll-Ups, 230
Salmon with Dijon Glaze, 116
Saskatoon Berry Custard Pie, 260
Scalloped Spaghetti Squash, 177
Scotch Eggs, 50
Shortbread Blackcurrant Crumble Bars, 262
Skinny Face Pizza Crust, 209
Sloppy Joe Burger, 151
Smoked Salmon Dip, 210
Southern Shore Cream Liqueur, 273
Southern-Fried Oven Chicken, 152
Spaniards Bay Spritzer, 273
Spanish Rice, 178
Sticky Kentucky Bourbon Chicken, 154
Sticky Toffee Pudding, 264
Stuffed Calamari Ring,s 53
Sweet 'n' Sour Meatballs, 157
Sweet Adorable Mustard Pickles, 200
Sylvia's Cherry Cake, 266

T

Thai Red Curry Noodles, 181
Tomato Parmesan Soup with Grilled Cheese, 96
Tomato-Butter Glazed Salmon, 119
Twice-Baked and Loaded Cauliflower, 182

V

Veal Parmesan, 158
Vinegar Pork Chops, 161

W

Warm German Faux-Tato Salad, 184
White Forest Cake, 268
Wraps, Wontons, and Fine Pastry, 213